LIVING BEYOND THE ORDINARY

Discovering the Keys to an Abundant Life

A Study of John

Jack W. Hayford
with
William D. Watkins

THOMAS NELSON PUBLISHERS
Nashville

CONTENTS

Living Beyond the Ordinary: Discovering the Keys to an Abundant Life (A Study of John) is one of a series of study guides that focus exciting, discovery-geared coverage of Bible book and power themes—all prompting toward dynamic, Holy Spirit-filled living.

About the General Editor

JACK W. HAYFORD, noted pastor, teacher, writer, and composer, is the General Editor of the complete series, working with the publisher in the conceiving and developing of each of the books.

Dr. Hayford is Senior Pastor of The Church On The Way, the First Foursquare Church of Van Nuys, California. He and his wife, Anna, have four married children, all of whom are active in either pastoral ministry or vital church life. As General Editor of the *Spirit-Filled Life Bible,* Pastor Hayford led a four-year project, which has resulted in the availability of one of today's most practical and popular study Bibles. He is author of more than twenty books, including *A Passion for Fullness, The Beauty of Spiritual Language, Rebuilding the Real You,* and *Prayer Is Invading the Impossible.* His musical compositions number over four hundred songs, including the widely sung "Majesty."

About the Writer

WILLIAM D. WATKINS has been integrally involved in Christian ministry since 1975 as teacher, writer, and speaker. Formerly with Insight for Living and Thomas Nelson Publishers, he is currently Senior Acquisitions Editor with Moody Press and president of his own literary company, William Pens. He coauthored *Worlds Apart: A Handbook on World Views,* published by Baker Book House; at Insight for Living, he coauthored twenty-one guides with Chuck Swindoll.

Bill has a B.A. in Philosophy from California State University at Fresno and a Th.M. in Systematic Theology from Dallas Theological Seminary. He and his wife, Pamela, have five children, ages 11–19. They reside in Smyrna, Tennessee.

Of this contributor, the General Editor has remarked: "Bill Watkins manifests such an even-handedness in his opening of the Scriptures, it is satisfying to be assisted by his work in this project. His longtime experience *in* the Word, along with his obvious love *for* God's Word, is a benefit to us all."

THE GIFT
THAT KEEPS ON GIVING

Who doesn't like presents? Whether they come wrapped in colorful paper and beautiful bows, or brown paper bags closed and tied at the top with old shoestring. Kids and adults of all ages love getting and opening presents.

But even this moment of surprise and pleasure can be marked by dread and fear. All it takes is for these words to appear: "Assembly Required. Instructions Enclosed." How we hate these words! They taunt us, tease us, beckon us to try to challenge them, all the while knowing that they have the upper hand. If we don't understand the instructions, or if we ignore them and try to put the gift together ourselves, more than likely, we'll only assemble frustration and anger. What we felt about our great gift—all the joy, anticipation, and wonder—will vanish. And they will never return, at least not to that pristine state they had before we realized that *we* had to assemble our present with instructions *no consumer* will ever understand.

One of the most precious gifts God has given us is His Word, the Bible. Wrapped in the glory and sacrifice of His Son and delivered by the power and ministry of His Spirit, it is a treasured gift—one the family of God has preserved and protected for centuries as a family heirloom. It promises that it is the gift that keeps on giving, because the Giver it reveals is inexhaustible in His love and grace.

Tragically, though, fewer and fewer people, even those who number themselves among God's everlasting family, are opening this gift and seeking to understand what it's all about and how to use it. They often feel intimidated by it. It requires some assembly, and its instructions are hard to comprehend sometimes. How does the Bible fit together anyway? What does Genesis have to do with Revelation? Who are Abraham and Moses, and what is their relationship to Jesus and Paul? And what about the works of the Law and the works of faith? What are they all about, and how do they fit together, if at all?

And what does this ancient book have to say to us who are looking toward the twenty-first century? Will taking the time and energy to understand its instructions and to fit it all together really help you and me? Will it help us better understand who we are, what the future holds, how we can better live here and now? Will it really help us in our personal relationships, in our marriages and families, in our jobs? Can it give us more than just advice on how to handle crises? the death of a loved one? the financial fallout of losing a job? catastrophic illness? betrayal by a friend? the seduction of our values? the abuses of the heart and soul? Will it allay our fears and calm our restlessness and heal our wounds? Can it really get us in touch with the same power that gave birth to the universe? that parted the Red Sea? that raised Jesus from the stranglehold of the grave? Can we really find unconditional love, total forgiveness, and genuine healing in its pages?

Yes. Yes. Without a shred of doubt.

The *Spirit-Filled Life Bible Discovery Guide* series is designed to help you unwrap, assemble, and enjoy all God has for you in the pages of Scripture. It will focus your time and energy on the books of the Bible, the people and places they describe, and the themes and life applications that flow thick from its pages like honey oozing from a beehive.

So you can get the most out of God's Word, this series has a number of helpful features. Each study guide has no more than fourteen lessons, each arranged so you can plumb the depths or skim the surface, depending on your needs and interests.

The study guides also contain six major lesson features, each marked by a symbol and heading for easy identification.

WORD WEALTH

The WORD WEALTH feature provides important definitions of key terms.

BEHIND THE SCENES

BEHIND THE SCENES supplies information about cultural beliefs and practices, doctrinal disputes, business trades, and the like that illuminate Bible passages and teachings.

 ### AT A GLANCE

The AT A GLANCE feature uses maps and charts to identify places and simplify themes or positions.

 ### BIBLE EXTRA

Because this study guide focuses on a book of the Bible, you will find a BIBLE EXTRA feature that guides you into Bible dictionaries, Bible encyclopedias, and other resources that will enable you to glean more from the Bible's wealth if you want something extra.

 ### PROBING THE DEPTHS

Another feature, PROBING THE DEPTHS, will explain controversial issues raised by particular lessons and cite Bible passages and other sources to which you can turn to help you come to your own conclusions.

 ### FAITH ALIVE

Finally, each lesson contains a FAITH ALIVE feature. Here the focus is, So what? Given what the Bible says, what does it mean for my life? How can it impact my day-to-day needs, hurts, relationships, concerns, and whatever else is important to me? FAITH ALIVE will help you see and apply the practical relevance of God's literary gift.

As you'll see, these guides supply space for you to answer the study and life-application questions and exercises. You may, however, want to record all your answers, or just the overflow from your study or application, in a separate notebook or journal. This would be especially helpful if you think you'll dig into the BIBLE EXTRA features. Because the exercises in this feature are optional and they can be expanded as far as you want to take them, we have not allowed writing space for them in this study guide. So you may want to have a notebook or journal handy for recording your discoveries while working through to this feature's riches.

The Bible study method used in this series revolves around four basic steps: observation, interpretation, correlation, and application. Observation answers the question, What does the text say? Interpretation deals with, What does the text mean?—not with what it means to you or me, but what it meant to its original readers. Correlation asks, What light do other Scripture passages shed on this text? And application, the goal of Bible study, poses the question, How should my life change in response to the Holy Spirit's teaching of this text?

If you have used a Bible much before, you know that it comes in a variety of translations and paraphrases. Although you can use any of them with profit as you work through the *Spirit-Filled Life Bible Discovery Guide* series, when Bible passages or words are cited, you will find they are from the New King James Version of the Bible. Using this translation with this series will make your study easier, but it's certainly not necessary.

The only resources you need to complete and apply these study guides are a heart and mind open to the Holy Spirit, a prayerful attitude, and a pencil and a Bible. Of course, you may draw upon other sources, such as commentaries, dictionaries, encyclopedias, atlases, and concordances, and you'll even find some optional exercises that will guide you into these sources. But these are extras, not necessities. These study guides are comprehensive enough to give you all you need to gain a good, basic understanding of the Bible book being covered and how you can apply its themes and counsel to your life.

A word of warning, though. By itself, Bible study will not transform your life. It will not give you power, peace, joy, comfort, hope, and a number of other gifts God longs for you to unwrap and enjoy. Through Bible study, you will grow in your understanding of the Lord, His kingdom and your place in it, and those things are essential. But you need more. You need to rely on the Holy Spirit to guide your study and your application of the Bible's truths. He, Jesus promised, was sent to teach us "all things" (John 14:26; cf. 1 Cor. 2:13). So as you use this series to guide you through Scripture, bathe your study time in prayer, asking the Spirit of God to illuminate the text, enlighten your mind, humble your will, and comfort your heart. He will never let you down.

My prayer and goal for you is that as you unwrap and begin to explore God's Book for living His way, the Holy Spirit will fill every fiber of your being to the joy and power God longs to give all His children. So read on. Be diligent. Stay open and submissive to Him. You will not be disappointed. He promises you!

Lesson 1/ The Beloved Disciple and His Gospel

You're friends. Best friends. She knows it, and you do, too.

You tell each other everything. You've told her that flying scares you so much that after you get off a flight you sit in the airport lobby until the strength flows back into your legs. She's told you her secret desire to become a famous race-car driver—a desire she hasn't told anyone about for years because those she told before laughed at her. You know who scoffed at her plans and how much they hurt her. You also know where she has begun to take private driving lessons in an attempt to see her dream come true. She knows who first kissed you, why you won't go for a walk by yourself anymore, how your father embarrassed you in front of your first date, when you've actually entertained the idea of shaving your husband's head bald while he's sleeping to get back at him for teasing you about your hair. You know why it's so hard for her to trust men anymore, how afraid she is of needles, why she slyly chuckles every time she eats jamoca almond fudge ice cream, and what the real meaning is behind one of her favorite phrases. Nothing is too sacred to share between you.

You've experienced every emotion together—riotous laughter, feelings of revenge, the disappointment of broken dreams, the hurts of innuendos and rumors, the frustrations of raising children who don't seem to appreciate you, much less listen to you.

You've been together for years. You've traveled together, vacationed together, worked on the same projects, tackled the same department store sales, shared the same movies, read each other's books.

If any two people have ever really known each other, you two do.

Then, your friend dies. You both saw it coming; it wasn't sudden. But she prepared for it much better than you did. In fact, when she died, you felt as though your entire body had been squeezed into your heart; then both were crushed with brutal, unrelenting blows.

How can you preserve her memory? What can you do to let others know what she was like, what she thought and felt and why, how much she meant to you? You begin to write. You reach back into your memories and start to record all you remember. You want to remember everything—as it was. Yes, you loved her, and you still do. But you want to make your portrait of her true to life, not glazed over with false eulogies; your relationship was based on truth, so you want to ensure that your account is, too. When you're done, you plan to share your written remembrances with others who could benefit from seeing your dearest friend, your best friend, as she really was.

Have you ever had a friend you cared for this much? John did. His name was Jesus. He had been born in Bethlehem and raised in Nazareth. The son of a carpenter (some said conceived illegitimately), Jesus became an itinerant preacher, spreading His message about the kingdom of God throughout first-century Palestine. That's when John met Him, joined up with His small band of followers, and grew to love Him as a best friend. Jesus felt the same way about John, and John knew He did (as we'll see later).

Traveling together, they swapped stories, shared secrets, learned what made each other angry and sad, found out what each liked to eat, encouraged each other, prayed for each other, and had words with each other. They knew each other as best friends do, but they both knew that, in spite of all they had in common, there were two things they didn't share. These two things made Jesus absolutely unique; no other human being had them, and, as His possessions, they made Him superior to every human being, living or dead. *He was God in the flesh and completely without sin.* Nothing in John's experience could have prepared him for a close relationship with such a man. The ecstasy of it all was indescribable.

But as awed as John could be in Jesus' presence, he could also feel Jesus' pain. Jesus knew He was going to die, and John knew it, too. He also knew that Jesus would suffer a great deal before His death, and that hurt him deeply.

John experienced the loss of his best friend—he even watched Him die. But he also saw Him a victor over death, and he dedicated the rest of his days to telling others about his best friend so they could become His friends, too. That's what John's gospel is all about. It is an intimate, realistic, yet mind-stretching portrayal of the man who shook the world. John's best friend, the Son of God, the Son of Man.

In this chapter, we want to learn some more about John, why he wrote his gospel, when and where he wrote it, and who may have been its first recipients. We also want to look at his portrait of Jesus as a whole. In later chapters, we'll have plenty of opportunities to examine the details.

As you begin this study, don't forget that this gospel is the product of love: John's love for Jesus, Jesus' love for you and me, and the Father's love for His Son and the world. In such a love letter, we'll find plenty that will apply to our lives, our relationships, our values, our joys, our pains.

JOHN, THE AUTHOR

As you read the Gospel of John, you won't find anyone identifying himself by name as its author. The same is true with the other three gospels—Matthew, Mark, and Luke. But two sources of evidence point to John as the Fourth Gospel's author.

The first source is *internal*—what the text of the gospel reveals about its author. A figure referred to as "the disciple whom Jesus loved" appears often throughout the gospel. And while most of the other twelve disciples of Jesus are named, this one is not; and one of the unnamed disciples is John. So by the process of elimination, the internal evidence leads to the conclusion that "the disciple whom Jesus loved" is John.

The second source of evidence is *external*, which deals with what church tradition claims about the gospel's author-ship. And this tradition consistently presents John, one of the sons of Zebedee, as the author of the Fourth Gospel. One of these historical sources, Irenaeus, who was the bishop of Lyons in the latter half of the second century and an associate of Polycarp who had known John, heard Polycarp testify that the Lord's disciple John published the Gospel of John while he was living in Ephesus.[1]

So the evidence is quite strong that John, the beloved disciple of the Lord, wrote the gospel that bears his name. (By the way, he also wrote 1, 2, and 3 John, and The Revelation.)

More about John can be gleaned from the New Testament. Look up the passages that follow to see what you can learn about him.

Mark 1:19

Matt. 4:21; Luke 5:10

Matt. 27:56; Mark 15:40 (cf. John 19:25)

John 1:35–42

John 2:2

Matt. 4:19–21

Mark 3:17; Luke 9:54

Matt. 17:1

John 13:23

John 19:26, 27

Acts 3:1–11

Acts 4:5–21

Acts 8:14–25

Gal. 2:9

1 John 1:1–4

Rev. 1:9

 FAITH ALIVE

From what you've discovered about John, what stands out to you about him? Do you see some traits that you wish were true about you? Write your answers here, then ask the Lord to begin working in your life to make these traits marks of your life of faith.

THE GOSPEL'S RECIPIENTS AND PURPOSE

Several of the New Testament books indicate for whom they were originally written. Romans was composed for the believers in Rome, while 1 and 2 Corinthians were written to address concerns at the church in Corinth. The Gospel of John does not indicate its readers like this. Although it clearly expresses a concern for the Jewish people outside the land of Israel (1:41; 4:25; 7:35; 10:16; 11:52; 20:31), its tone is more universal, including Gentile Christians and all unbelievers. It was written, says John, "that you may believe that Jesus is the Christ, the Son of God, and that believing you may have life in His name" (20:31). So this is a book for anyone who needs

Jesus or needs to deepen their relationship with Him. You can't get much broader than that.

WHEN AND WHERE

While some Bible scholars date the composition of John's gospel around or before A.D. 70, most put it between A.D. 85 and 90, or at least prior to the close of the first century.[2]

Church tradition, as we have already noted, says that this gospel was written by John in the city of Ephesus.

BIBLE EXTRA

Read the Ephesians letter in the New Testament and see what else you can discover about Ephesus and the church there by checking out some Bible dictionaries or encyclopedias. You'll quickly see how tough it could be to be a Christian in pagan Ephesus.

FAITH ALIVE

It's not unusual to hear people complain about how hard it is to be a Christian in their community. Do you do that? What have you gleaned so far in this study that should perhaps work to change your attitude and perspective?

How about it? Are you willing to be changed?

THE GOSPEL'S MESSAGE

If you have ever read the synoptic Gospels—Matthew, Mark, and Luke—you know that they have a lot of similar content, and they basically present the same chronology of Jesus' life and ministry, death and resurrection. The Gospel of John is much different. Its arrangement is more topical than chronological. And when a chronology presents itself, it's wrapped around the Jewish religious calendar, showing Jesus at many of the major religious festivals generating controversy over who He claims to be and what He does. Turn to the texts listed below and jot down what religious celebration Jesus is attending and what happens when He does.

2:13–25

5:1–18

6:4–15

7:2–52

10:22–39

11:55—12:43

13:1–5

18:1—19:42

 FAITH ALIVE

Do you think Christians should stay on the shore and not create any waves? Jesus didn't think so. His example makes it clear that He was willing to move into a situation and stir things up—not for controversy's sake, but for the stirring of interest and for the spread of God's kingdom. When was the last time the expression of your faith generated some holy commotion? If it's been a long time, you may need to engage in some self-reflection to discover why. Feel free to write your thoughts here.

FAITH ALIVE

With this background information in mind, it's time to read through the entire gospel and get a closer look at John's portrait of Jesus. You might make it a project for this week to read three chapters daily and develop your own brief paragraph summaries for each day's coverage. A half hour per day will allow this fruitful overview and set you in good stead for the following seasons of study.

In your overview of John, what made a deep impression on you?

Why do you think these things stuck out to you?

Take some time right now to bring these things before God. Request that He show you the significance of these matters and what He desires to teach you through them. Consider also your willingness to allow change in your life in these areas. If you're reluctant, bring the Lord in on that, too.

1. Irenaeus, *Against Heresies* 3.1.1, as cited in F. F. Bruce, *The Gospel of John* (Grand Rapids, MI: William B. Eerdmans Publishing Company, 1983), 11.

2. See John A. T. Robinson, *Redating the New Testament* (Philadelphia, PA: Westminster Press, 1976), chap. 9; Merrill C. Tenney, "The Gospel of John," in *The Expositor's Bible Commentary*, gen. ed. Frank E. Gaebelein (Grand Rapids, MI: Zondervan Publishing House, 1981), 9:9, 10.

Lesson 2/The God-Man (1:1–18)

Christianity is Christ. Many of the world's religions believe in one God. Almost all of them believe that humankind is in trouble and needs to be saved somehow. And most think that at least one judgment awaits us—a judgment based on what we do during our sojourn on earth. But only Christianity teaches that Jesus Christ is the key that unlocks all the doors essential to our past, our present, and our future. Only Christianity views Jesus as the sole mediator between God and people. Only Christianity sees Jesus as the world's only real hope for salvation—a salvation based on grace and mercy through faith, not on self-reliance or education or information control or behavior modification or community or any other lesser good.

Why is this so? Why is Christianity so adamant about the central role of Jesus Christ? Because Jesus Christ is God in the flesh. This man, born in Bethlehem and raised in Nazareth by Mary and Joseph, is also fully God. While being cradled in Mary's arms as a baby, He was sustaining the entire universe in existence. While feeding at Mary's breasts, He was providing nourishing rains all over the earth. While learning the trade of carpentry at Joseph's side, He was being worshiped and adored by angels. This man who ate, grew tired, became frustrated, voiced anger, perspired, suffered, cried, was misunderstood and rejected—this man was also deity—in need of nothing, in control of everything, all-powerful, all-knowing, all-loving, perfect in every way. He is the God-man: Everything that belongs to deity, He has; everything that belongs to humanity, except for sin, He has. Fully God yet fully man. Only Christianity affirms this truth about Jesus. So central is it that if Christianity is wrong about Jesus, then

Christianity is false. Christianity is Christ. Without Him, Christianity has nothing unique to say, nothing unique to give, no hope to offer, no forgiveness to promise, no salvation that can be secured, no Son, no Spirit, no Father, no nothing.

John, the human author of the Fourth Gospel, knows this fact very well. So in his gospel's prologue, which is made up of the first eighteen verses, he sets out the basic facts about Jesus—who He is, what He is, why He came to earth, and why we should listen to Him and not turn away. The facts presented are startling, revolutionary, heart-stirring. But more than that, they can be life-giving, at least for those who have ears to hear, wills to obey.

So before we delve any deeper, take a few minutes to read John 1:1–18 a couple of times.

PARALLELS TO PONDER

Correlation is one of the most illuminating steps of Bible study. When you use correlation, you compare passages in one part of the Bible to similar passages in another part. This process ends up throwing light on both sets of passages, so you walk away with a better understanding of the meaning of the texts.

When you read John 1:1—"In the beginning was the Word"—you may have noticed that it begins like Genesis 1:1: "In the beginning God created the heavens and the earth." As you read a little further into John 1, you may have also noticed that it talks about the Word's involvement in creation, which also brings to mind the creation account of Genesis 1.

Read Genesis 1:1—2:4, then reread John 1:1–18. See what parallels of wording, ideas, and structural arrangement you can find between the two passages.

The message of John 1:12b is the one the prologue's whole structure is pointing to; it's the climax at the end of the crescendo. And when we see the prologue as the message of the entire gospel in miniature, then what would you say is the main idea of John's gospel? How does your answer square with John 20:31?

Why do you think John was so careful to allude to the beginning of Genesis in content and structure? What was he trying to get across?

 FAITH ALIVE

When you recall that God inspired the Bible, that the words of the human authors are ultimately His words, the incredible literary structure in which those words find their bedding speaks volumes about the emphasis God places on design and the beauty He brings within it. Take some time to ponder this and record your thoughts here. For instance: What does this tell you about the rest of God's works? Should we embrace or reject chaos or reckless unconcern for order in worship services or business meetings? Does God's use of foundational structure allow room for spontaneity and creativity? I'm sure you can think of some other questions and issues to explore.

Now let's probe more deeply into John's prologue.

NO GOD BUT GOD

In John 1:1–3, two truths are established: (1) the Word is God; (2) the Word is in some way different from God. What in these verses supports the first truth?

What supports the second truth?

Who is the Word (cf. vv. 14, 17)?

How do you think the Word can be the same as God, yet different? You may want to consult the "Word Wealth" section below before trying to answer this question.

WORD WEALTH

In the beginning (1:1, 2): This phrase refers to the start of creation, harking back to Genesis 1:1.

Was (1:1): Indicates that the Word predates the start of creation. In other words, the Word was in existence prior to even the first act of bringing the universe into being.

With (1:1): Toward God, face to face with God, in company with God. The idea is that the Word was in eternal fellowship with the rest of the Godhead—God the Father and God the Holy Spirit.

God (1:1, 2): In the first and third occurrences of this word, *God* refers to the Father and the Holy Spirit (the first and third members of the Godhead). The second use of the term means "deity"; it indicates the indivisible divine nature that the Word shares with the Father and the Holy Spirit.

Word (1:1): The English translation of the Greek term *logos*. To the first-century Jewish mind, *logos* meant the spoken word, with the emphasis on the meaning, not the sound, of the word, so it would imply a personal being involved in communication. Because of the similarity between John 1:1 and Genesis 1:1, Jewish readers would have connected the *Word* in John with the creative activity of God in Genesis 1, where He spoke and things came into being (Gen. 1:3). So for them, *Logos* would designate the personal creative power and activity of God. It is word in action.

For Greek readers, *logos* meant "reason, rational thought, and discourse; the principle of reason or order in the world that gives the world its form and makes up the soul of man." We get our word *logic* from *logos*.

Together, these meanings tell us that the Word is the personal, rational source of power and action in creation. The apostle John undoubtedly chose this word so it would appeal to Jews and Greeks, conveying truths both groups would associate with the Word.[1]

Nothing (1:3): Not even one thing was made apart from the creative work of the Word.[2]

BEHIND THE SCENES

The Fourth Gospel begins with one of the most difficult doctrines in Christianity—the Trinity. When John talks about the sameness between the Word and God, yet also indicates difference, he raises a problem that Christians have always accepted but took a few hundred years to resolve. The Bible makes it very clear that there is only one God (Deut. 6:4; Is. 44:6–8; 45:5, 6, 18, 21, 22; 1 Cor. 8:4–6; 1 Tim. 2:5). But the Bible also clearly states that the Father is God (John 6:27; Rom. 1:7; Gal. 1:1), Jesus Christ is God (John 1:1–3, 14; Col. 2:9; Titus 2:13; Heb. 1:2, 3; 1 John 5:20), and the Holy Spirit is God (Acts 5:3, 4; 28:25–27; 2 Cor. 3:16, 17; Heb. 10:15, 16). Furthermore, the Bible ascribes divine attributes and activities to two or all three of these Persons in the same context (Matt. 28:18, 19; 1 Cor. 1:3; 2 Cor. 13:14; Eph. 4:4–6).

Faced with these biblical passages and numerous others, the fourth-century church eventually formally articulated the relationship between the Father, the Son, and the Holy Spirit as three uncreated, eternal, coequal Persons coexisting in or sharing the same indivisible divine nature. Therefore, each Person is fully God, possessing exactly the same divine attributes because each shares exactly the same nature, yet each Person is eternally distinct—the Father is not the Son or the Spirit, the Son is not the Father or the Spirit, and the Spirit is not the Father or the Son. In short, there is only one God, but this God is three distinct Persons eternally coexisting in one divine nature.

If you find this difficult to understand, be of good cheer—you're not alone! Shouldn't the God of all the universe be "slightly" beyond our description, seeing He is God? In submitting to faith, know that throughout the centuries the church has upheld this understanding of God as a faithful description of what the Bible teaches. Truly great minds are consistently willing to acknowledge their finite grasp and to leave room for the "possibility" that the transcendent greatness of God "might" exceed their full grasp. Yet still, in the personal nature of His love He has chosen to reveal Himself to us. (See the end of this chapter for some resources that can help you plumb some of the depths of this inexhaustible topic.)

LIFE AND LIGHT

In John 1:1, 2, the Word is God. In verse 3, the Word is the Creator. In verses 4–13, what is the Word?

Who was sent from God before the Word, and why was he sent? (vv. 6–8)

Where did the Word go, and how was He received? (vv. 5, 11, 12)

John tells us that the Word is the light. What is the darkness?

What are the stated ironies in verses 9–11?

Know (1:10): "The recognition of truth by personal experience."[3]

What do these ironies tell you about the condition of our world and how we can expect people to respond to Jesus?

What do you think verses 12 and 13 are teaching about how we are saved and not saved? Put another way, what are these verses saying about the *means* of salvation (the way by which we are saved as opposed to the ways we are not saved) and the *source* of salvation (who saves us and who cannot)?

WORD WEALTH

Right (1:12): Authority.

Become children of God (1:12): Apart from Christ, we don't start out as part of God's forever family. We must come into it, and when we do, we come in as His adopted little ones.

Believe in His name (1:12): An active commitment to Jesus Christ—His person, His character, His work.

Born (1:13): A figure of speech used to signify spiritual, not physical, birth into God's family (cf. John 3:1–21).

FAITH ALIVE

Do you understand who saves you and how? Are you clear about God's role and yours? If not, reread John's prologue and review this chapter of the study guide. If need be, get together with your pastor, a Bible teacher, or a Christian friend and ask one of them to explain it to you. Whatever you do, don't let this important information slip by you. Your eternal destiny may hang in the balance.

THE WORD INCARNATE

Before the Word came, God had revealed Himself in the world in a variety of ways throughout history (Heb. 1:1). What were some of these ways?

What made the revelation of God in the Word unique? (John 1:14, 17, 18)

Given all the ways God manifested Himself in the Old Testament, how can John say that no one has ever seen the Father, that only the Son has revealed Him? (v. 18) How can you explain this? (We will deal with this issue in more detail later in this study, but for now, do your best to resolve this apparent problem.)

What did John the Baptist say about the Word incarnate? (v. 15)

  WORD WEALTH

The Word became flesh (1:14): The Word, the Son of God, took to Himself a fully human nature (body, soul, and spirit), one just like ours yet untainted by sin, so He now had two distinct natures—one fully human and another fully divine.

Dwelt (1:14): Pitched His tent. The dwelling place of God among His people was no longer the tabernacle or temple (Ex. 25:8; 40:34; 1 Kin. 8:10–12), but the incarnate Son of God.

Glory (1:14): "The manifestation of God, the outward shining of His inward being,"[4] like the rays of sunlight manifest the presence and power of their source, the sun. In this way Jesus revealed the magnificence of deity through His humanity.

Begotten of the Father (1:14): This does not refer to Christ's earthly conception or birth but to the unique, eternal, loving relationship He has with the heavenly Father as His Son.

Grace for grace (1:16): One wave of grace being constantly replaced by another one. Grace heaped on grace; grace overflowing.[5]

Law (1:17): The revelation of God that came through the prophet Moses. Although God's grace and truth were seen in the Law, they have been manifested in Jesus Christ in such fullness that there is hardly any comparison between the two revelations.

 ## BEHIND THE SCENES

Once again, John introduces one of the most difficult Christian teachings—the Incarnation. Like the doctrine of the Trinity, the doctrine of the Incarnation took some time to develop formally, even though the church always accepted the fact that Jesus was both human and divine at the same time. In the fourth century, however, at two major church councils—one at Nicea and the other at Chalcedon—the church settled this issue.

The church declared that the Second Person of the Trinity—the Son—added a full-blown human nature (minus any actual sin or any propensity to sin) to His deity, yet without changing anything in the divine nature. So while remaining fully God and without any alterations to His deity, the Son joined Himself to a real human nature in the virgin womb of Mary. And due to the distinctions among the three Persons of the Godhead, only the Son became incarnate; neither the Father nor the Holy Spirit took to themselves a human nature. So the Son, and the Son alone, is fully divine in one nature and fully human in another nature. And these two natures, though joined in one Person, do not mix characteristics (for example, the human nature can't become all-powerful, and the divine nature can't grow weak) nor are they separated from one another. Therefore Jesus Christ is one Person possessing two distinct natures that make Him in every way the unique God-man. (See the end of this chapter for some reading suggestions on this topic.)

 ## PROBING THE DEPTHS

As we saw earlier, the doctrines of the Trinity and the Incarnation have been tough for the church to nail down, and they are still difficult to understand. So you can get a better grip on them, I have listed some resources here that will give you some helpful historical background, provide illustrations and explanations, answer some common objections, and show how biblical and reasonable these two doctrines really are. You can't plumb the depths of these doctrines without reaping personal benefits, so go ahead—dive in. It will be well worth your time and effort.

The Trinity
Bowman, Robert M., Jr. *Why You Should Believe in the Trinity: An Answer to Jehovah's Witnesses.* Grand Rapids, MI: Baker Book House, 1989.

Beisner, E. Calvin. *God in Three Persons.* Wheaton, IL: Tyndale House Publishers, 1984.

Bickersteth, Edward Henry. *The Trinity.* Reprint ed. Grand Rapids, MI: Kregel Publications, 1984.

Fortman, Edmund J. *The Triune God: A Historical Study of the Doctrine of the Trinity.* Grand Rapids, MI: Baker Book House, 1972.

Wainwright, Arthur W. *The Trinity in the New Testament.* London, England: SPCK, 1962.

Wood, Nathan R. *The Trinity in the Universe.* Grand Rapids, MI: Kregel Publications, 1978.

The Incarnation
Athanasius, Saint. *On the Incarnation.* Reprint ed. Crestwood, NY: St. Vladimir's Orthodox Theological Seminary, 1982.

Bray, Gerald. *Creeds, Councils, and Christ.* Downers Grove, IL: InterVarsity Press, 1984.

Kelly, J. N. D. *Early Christian Doctrines.* Revised ed. San Francisco, CA: Harper & Row, 1978.

Morris, Thomas V. *The Logic of God Incarnate.* Ithaca, NY: Cornell University Press, 1986.

Norris, Richard A., Jr., trans. and ed. *The Christological Controversy.* Sources of Early Christian Thought series. Philadelphia, PA: Fortress Press, 1980.

Walvoord, John F. *Jesus Christ Our Lord.* Chicago, IL: Moody Press, 1969.

Wells, David F. *The Person of Christ.* Foundations for Faith series. Westchester, IL: Crossway Books, 1984.

1. Merrill C. Tenney, "The Gospel of John," in *The Expositor's Bible Commentary,* gen. ed. Frank E. Gaebelein (Grand Rapids, MI: Zondervan Publishing House, 1981), 9:28; Fritz Reinecker, *Linguistic Key to the Greek New Testament,* ed. Cleon L. Rogers, Jr. (Grand Rapids, MI: Zondervan Publishing House, 1980), 217; Gordon H. Clark, "The Axiom of Revelation," in *The Philosophy of Gordon H. Clark,* ed. Ronald H. Nash (Philadelphia, PA: The Presbyterian and Reformed Publishing Company, 1968), 67.

2. F. F. Bruce, *The Gospel of John* (Grand Rapids, MI: William B. Eerdmans Publishing Company, 1983), 32.

3. *Spirit-Filled Life Bible* (Nashville, TN: Thomas Nelson Publishers, 1991), "Word Wealth: 8:32 know," 1589.

4. Ibid., 1694, note on 5:2.

5. Bruce, *The Gospel of John,* 42.

Lesson 3/Who Are You?
(1:19—2:25)

Imagine a place where people had the same name and the same job. Everyone looked, dressed, and behaved alike. Their homes were identical inside and out. Their cars had no distinguishing features. Indeed, nothing about them set them apart from each other except their sex and the amount of space each person took up. Sounds horrible, doesn't it? None of us would want to live in such an awful place.

At times, of course, we may wish we had someone else's name, looks, celebrity status, talent, or material goods. Sometimes we may even wish we had been born somewhere else or into another family. But these occasional desires are usually overridden by a greater, more basic need to have our own identities, to be our own persons. Every parent who has an adolescent knows how strong this urge is. While we want to fit in and belong, we don't want to become absorbed by others (though that happens to us occasionally). We want to stand out from the crowd, even lead the crowd. We want to carve out and retain our own identities.

Why is this drive so strong? Because God designed us this way. "I want to be me" is not the refrain of egotism but of individuals created in God's image who long to discover who they are and fulfill their life's purpose. People don't always understand this about themselves, but that doesn't discount the fact that God has designed them to pursue self-discovery and self-fulfillment.

In John 1:19—2:25, you'll learn about a man who was sure about who he was and his calling. You'll also meet four other people who began to discover what God had created them to do with their lives. Regardless of how far you have come in understanding yourself and your life purpose, this portion of John can help you move even closer to grasping these basic, God-ordained goals.

JOHN KNOWS JOHN

John 1:19–28 deals with John the Baptist and some people who are intensely interested in his identity and purpose.

Where was John, and what was he doing? (vv. 25, 28)

Who went out to see John, and where were they from? (vv. 19, 24)

 BEHIND THE SCENES

Throughout the Fourth Gospel, we'll see many groups come question or accuse Jesus. Here we see three Jewish religious groups involved: the priests, Levites, and Pharisees (vv. 19, 24).

The words *the Jews* refer at times to the people of Israel as a whole or to Judeans as distinct from Galileans (7:1), but in this part of the gospel they designate the religious establishment in Jerusalem. This body of religious leaders sent a delegation of priests, Levites, and Pharisees to question John the Baptist.

The priests were the theological authorities. Descendants of Aaron, their primary job was to minister at the altar in the temple (Ex. 28:1).

The Levites were descendants of Levi, and they had been appointed to assist the priests with the temple ritual and service (Num. 8:19, 26).

Unlike the priests and Levites, whose beginnings were instituted by God in the Old Testament Law, the Pharisees came on the scene at the end of the second century B.C. The Pharisees believed that the written and oral traditions of the rabbis were as authoritative as the written Law of Moses. The rabbis' traditions were basically theological and practical commentaries on the Mosaic Law, and they were developed to ensure that the Law's principles would remain applicable to the changes of Jewish society. By preserving and following these traditions, the Pharisees were trying to safeguard the Law from being dismissed as irrelevant or obsolete.

The name *Pharisees* means "separated ones," and that's how the members of this group were best known. In their religious devotion, they separated themselves from everything that might convey or lead to ethical or ceremonial impurity. According to the Jewish historian Josephus, himself a follower of their principles, the Pharisees had the reputation of "excelling the rest of their nation in the observances of religion, and as exact exponents of the laws" (*Jewish Wars* 1.110). They were an influential minority among the Jewish religious leaders during the days of Jesus.[1]

Who did John the Baptist say he was not? (John 1:20, 21)

Who did John the Baptist say he was, and how was his identity connected with his mission? (vv. 23, 26, 27; cf. Is. 40:3–5)

 **BEHIND THE SCENES**

John's denials are as important as his affirmation. If he had said he was the Christ, he would have identified himself with the One who had been prophesied to bring deliverance to Israel. The religious leaders could have reported this identity claim to the Romans, who would have viewed the claimant as a potential insurrectionist. Insurrection was punishable by death according to Roman law. What the Jews didn't realize is that John was paving the way for the expected Deliverer, who would eventually die at the hands of the Romans under the charge of insurrection (19:12–19).

The idea that John could have been Elijah was based on the promise that Elijah the prophet would come before the Messiah (cf. Mal. 4:5, 6). Even though John looked and sounded like the expected Elijah and had a ministry similar to his (Luke 1:13–17, 76–79), John still denied the identification. He came in Elijah's power and office, but he was not the resurrected prophet.

Many Jews also expected a prophet like Moses to arise before the Messiah's arrival (Deut. 18:15–19). They hoped this prophet would deliver them from their enemies in a new Exodus, and they expected him to be a separate individual from the Messiah. They were wrong on both counts. Jesus was the fulfillment of this Old Testament expectation, as John (and Philip) apparently knew (John 1:45), and He was not the Jews' political deliverer.

John knew who he was: the voice in the wilderness, the herald of the Lord, the way-preparer for the Messiah, the witness-bearer of the true Light. Because his self-identity and calling were sure in his mind, he could make them clear to others and be effective in his mission.

 ### FAITH ALIVE

Is your self-identity and life purpose clear to you? Can you say with John the Baptist, "I know who I am and am not, and I know what God has called me to do"? If so, specify your answer below, spelling out who you are and your calling. If not, turn your written response into a prayer, petitioning the Lord to help you define yourself and discover what He wants you to do for the spread of His kingdom.

The religious leaders didn't know who John was, and John told them that they didn't know whom he represented even though that Person was moving among them (1:26). How does all this relate to verses 10, 11?

FAITH ALIVE

Have you ever known people who are very religious, yet really don't know the Messiah, Jesus Christ? They may attend worship services, pray, and strictly observe a code of conduct, but they still don't know who Jesus is. Recall how John the Baptist dealt with such folks and, from his example, articulate some principles that can guide you in your dealings with religious agnostics.

JOHN KNOWS JESUS

John the Baptist's primary mission was to bear witness about Jesus. In John 1:29–34, what does the Baptist testify about Christ? Who does he say Jesus is, and what does he say Jesus came to do?

WORD WEALTH

The Lamb of God (1:29): In the Old Testament, lambs are connected to a number of sacrifices: the Passover (Ex. 12:3–14); the daily temple sacrifice (Ex. 29:38–41); the burnt offering (Lev. 1:10); the peace offering (3:7); the sin offering (4:32); purifying a leper (14:13); the Feast of Trumpets, Tabernacles, and Day of Atonement (Num. 29:1–40). All of these sacrifices are likely implied by the title "the Lamb of God." But because so much of the Fourth Gospel is developed around the Passover Feast, the Passover sacrifice may be the primary one in view. "The Passover taught that deliverance was effected through the shedding of blood—the death of the innocent in behalf of the guilty (Ex. 12:1–14). Jews hearing John speak would likely link his remark to the Passover lamb,"[2] concluding that John was claiming that Jesus was God's sacrificial lamb, who by shedding His blood would remove the world's sins (cf. 1 Cor. 5:7; Rev. 5:6–14).

The Son of God (1:34): This title expresses Jesus' divine nature (5:18), His unique relationship to God the Father (5:20; 6:47), and His special knowledge of the Father (10:15).

Witness (1:32): Also translated "testimony," this term occurs nearly fifty times in John's gospel. The apostle John uses it in two ways: (1) to indicate what is legally acceptable testimony to prove the truth of something (8:17), and (2) to show that a commitment has been made to that truth. The truth witnessed to is Jesus, and in the Fourth Gospel the witnesses are John the Baptist (1:6, 7, 34); a variety of other human beings, including the disciples (15:27) and the crowds who saw Jesus' incredible deeds (12:17); Jesus' own works (5:36; 10:25); Scripture (5:39); the Father (5:31, 32, 37); the Holy Spirit (15:26); and, of course, Jesus Himself (8:14, 18). The point is that there are more than enough witnesses to establish the truth about Jesus' identity and mission.[3]

 FAITH ALIVE

Are you sure about who Jesus is and what He did for you? Why or why not?

If someone asked you, "How do you know that Jesus is the Messiah, the Son of God?" what evidence could you provide as a witness?

John admits that although he sought to prepare the way of the Lord, he didn't know how he would recognize the Lord. How was that problem solved? (vv. 31, 33)

FAITH ALIVE

John the Baptist needed help to recognize Jesus. How do you recognize His presence in your life?

What can you do to help others identify Him?

What were the differences between John's baptism and Jesus'? (v. 33) Look up the passages listed below, then note in the appropriate column what they say about Jesus' baptism and John's.

Scriptures	Jesus' Baptism	John's Baptism
Ezek. 36:25–27		
Joel 2:28–30		
Matt. 3:11, 12		
Mark 1:4, 5		
Luke 24:49		
John 7:38, 39		
Acts 2:5–41		
Acts 19:1–6		
1 Cor. 12:13		

Have you been baptized in water as Jesus commanded? (Matt. 28:18–20) Tell what happened.

Have you been baptized in the Holy Spirit as Jesus promised? (Acts 1:5, 8) Tell what happened.

JESUS KNOWS US

When Jesus arrived on the scene, John the Baptist knew that his ministry would have to decrease and Jesus' would have to increase (cf. John 3:27–30). Soon after John baptized Jesus, he began telling his disciples to follow "the Lamb of God" (1:36).

Who were the first disciples to do this? (1:37, 40)

Who do you think the unnamed disciple is? Could it be John the apostle? What did we deal with in chapter 1 that could lead one to identify this person as the writer of the Fourth Gospel?

What question did Jesus ask them? (v. 38)

Why do you think Jesus focused on *what* rather than *who*? What does His choice of words tell you about what He was really asking them?

What was Jesus' answer to the disciples' question? (v. 38)

FAITH ALIVE

Jesus' answer to seekers is as relevant today as it was then. How might you apply that answer to evangelistic situations? Put the essence of Jesus' answer into your own words as if you were speaking to unbelieving seekers.

Andrew found his brother Simon and brought him to Jesus. What did Andrew say to Simon to get him to come along, and why would it have been important to Simon? (v. 41)

WORD WEALTH

Messiah (1:41): "In Hebrew, 'Messiah' means 'the anointed One,' which in Greek is translated *Christ*. . . . The idea of 'the anointed One' comes from the Old Testament practice of anointing priests and kings with oil. This was symbolic of the Spirit and pointed to the future One who would come (cf. Is. 61:1). The title 'Messiah' came to be used of the future Davidic King (cf. Matt. 1:1; John 6:15)."[4] As the "anointed One," Jesus' kingly role is noted, as well as His "Baptizer with the Holy Spirit" role (John 1:33) by which He passes His "kingdom anointing" on to those He fills with His

Spirit—the promise of power for ministry (Act1:8) and of truth for steadfastness (1 John 2:18–26).

When Simon met Jesus, Jesus changed Simon's name (John 1:42). What was the significance of the name change? For additional help, see Matthew 16:18; Luke 22:31, 32; John 21:15–19; Acts 2—5; 10—12.

Who was the first disciple Jesus called personally, and what did He tell him to do? (John 1:43)

What was this person's connection to Andrew and Peter? (v. 44)

Do you suppose Andrew and Peter told Jesus about him? Why or why not?

 FAITH ALIVE

Jesus' call to Philip is the same one He makes to all who choose to trust in Him by faith. Have you answered that call? Are you fulfilling it daily? What can you do this week to follow Him more closely, more surely?

What followed on the heels of Philip's commitment to follow Jesus? (vv. 45, 46)

FAITH ALIVE

When was the last time you sought out someone to tell him or her about Jesus? To whom can you go within the next couple of weeks? List those individuals here, then leave space beside each name so you can record what happened.

Nathanael's initial response to Philip didn't show a very high regard for Jesus' hometown (v. 46). Why do you think he held this opinion? (cf. 7:41, 42, 52)

What was so unusual about what Jesus did that led Nathanael to conclude that Jesus was "the Son of God" and "the King of Israel"? (v. 49; cf. vv. 47, 48, 50)

Jesus' closing words to Nathanael are reminiscent of Jacob's dream in Genesis 28:10–15. Why would Jesus allude to this event? What point was He making to Nathanael?

WORD WEALTH

Most assuredly, I say to you (1:51): A phrase of solemn affirmation meant to express certainty that what is said is trustworthy and will be fulfilled.[5]

THE ACTIONS OF ASSURANCE

Jesus could not have won the support of so many people so quickly unless He was self-assured about His identity as the Father's Son and His mission as the Father's chosen Savior. Jesus knew what He was all about; His actions and the responses He received revealed that. We saw the same thing with John the Baptist. You don't have to be God's Son to have that kind of assurance, but when you know you're rightly related to Him, following Him His way, that kind of assurance will come.

So keep looking to Him, as John and the other disciples did. The rest will take care of itself.

1. For more on the Pharisees, as well as the other religious groups in first-century Palestine, see F. F. Bruce, *New Testament History* (Garden City, NY: Doubleday & Company, 1969), and J. Robert Teringo, *The Land and People Jesus Knew* (Minneapolis, MN: Bethany House Publishers, 1985).

2. Taken from *John,* Moody Gospel Commentary, by J. Carl Laney; gen. ed. Paul Enns. Copyright 1992, Moody Bible Institute of Chicago Moody Press. Used by permission.

3. Leon Morris, *Reflections on the Gospel of John,* vol. 1 (Grand Rapids, MI: Baker Book House, 1986), 29, 30.

4. Edwin A. Blum, "John," in *The Bible Knowledge Commentary: New Testament Edition,* gen. eds. John F. Walvoord and Roy B. Zuck (Wheaton, IL: Victor Books, 1983), 275.

5. F. F. Bruce, *The Gospel of John,* (Grand Rapids, MI: William B. Eerdmans Publishing Company, 1983), 672.

Lesson 4/Life Everlasting a Messiah Away
(2:1—3:36)

- "Honey! My dream job came through! I'm on my way!"
- "My husband wanted a son. I know he's disappointed, but I think he'll adjust."
- "She had put in a lot of work toward purchasing that farm, but when her expected raise didn't come through, she had to abandon her plans."
- "He romanced her until he won her heart. I've never seen a happier groom!"
- "After her only daughter died in that car accident, she never forgave God. 'A good God would never have taken my Jessica away from me,' I heard her say. She died believing that."

Expectations. We all have them, and we order our lives around them. They motivate us, change us, challenge us, sometimes even disturb us. They can lift us up or let us down, crown us or trash us. Their fulfillment can elude us for years, even a lifetime. And yet at times they come to fruition faster than we could have ever hoped or feared. Often the way in which they finally become realities knocks us off our feet, like being tripped in the dark. Sometimes we jump back up with joy; sometimes we never stand as tall again; for some of us, the pain can be so great that we never even get up.

Among first-century Jewish people, the expectations for the Messiah who was to come were at an all-time high. The Jews were being ruled by Gentiles—Romans—and, understandably, they hated it. They longed to be out from under the heavy hand of the Roman Empire and so kept watch for a military Messiah, a political Deliverer (cf. Ps. 2; Is. 11; 12; Dan. 7).

Although some people looked to Jesus as their mighty Warrior-King, He would have none of it (John 6:14, 15). His mission and ways were different, which confused and disillusioned many of His Jewish contemporaries, even some of His disciples. Others felt threatened and tried to kill Him, and one of His own would betray Him. Some, however, would see in Him their salvation, and they would believe in Him and find it. All would view Him with expectations, and some would have their expectations fulfilled, while others would see them fall away.

Let's see how He measures up to your expectations.

SIGNS OF REVELATION

Excluding the resurrection and the miraculous catch of fish recorded in John 21:4–11, John records seven signs (miracles), each designed to reveal something about the Person of Christ, to authenticate His message, and to point to the future kingdom of the Messiah (cf. Is. 35:5, 6). The first of these signs is found in John 2, and we'll deal with it in more detail in just a bit. For now, read through the passages below, then jot down the sign and what it unveils about Jesus, His message, and/or His kingdom. This helps us see how "signs" are used by the Lord in His ministry, not as entertainment or gimmicks, but as demonstrations of deity to verify His supernatural presence and power.

THE SEVEN SIGNS

Scriptures	Signs	Significance
2:1–11		
4:46–54		
5:1–9		
6:1–14		
6:16–21		
9:1–12		
11:1–46		

SAVING THE BEST TILL LAST

The scene of the first sign takes place "in Cana of Galilee" (2:1), which was about seventy-five miles from Bethany, the place Jesus had been gathering His disciples (1:28), and about eight miles from His hometown of Nazareth. The occasion was a Jewish wedding feast that lasted anywhere from one to seven days, depending on the new husband's resources.[1] It was a time of tremendous joy and celebration; and Jesus, His disciples, and His mother had all been invited (2:1, 2).

In your own words, describe what happened, including what led up to the miracle, the miracle itself, and how people responded to it (vv. 3–11).

WORD WEALTH

My hour has not yet come (v. 4): This statement carries two meanings: (1) "It is not yet time for Me to act," which would refer to Jesus' looking for the appropriate moment to replenish the wine supply; (2) "It is not yet time for Me to be glorified," which, while happening to a degree after the miracle occurs (v. 11), still doesn't find its ultimate fulfillment until Jesus' crucifixion and resurrection (cf. 7:6–8, 30; 8:20; 12:23–33; 13:1; 16:32; 17:1).

FAITH ALIVE

Have you ever tried to rush things along? Perhaps you tried to develop a relationship too fast, or maybe you tried to pull together a project before you were fully prepared to handle it, or maybe you tried to hurry God along by presuming He would answer your prayer one way, only to discover that He had another plan altogether. All of us become impatient, presume too much, push too hard at times, but Jesus' example is that "To everything *there is* a season, a time for every purpose under heaven" (Eccl. 3:1). He moved in perfect synchronization with the Father.

How can you move out in God's timing rather than yours? List some ways below, then submit them to Him in prayer, asking Him to help you implement them with patient reliance on Him.

TAKING CARE OF BUSINESS

After leaving Cana and spending some time in Capernaum with His mother, brothers, and disciples, Jesus traveled to Jerusalem for the Passover (John 2:12, 13).

 ### WORD WEALTH

Brothers (2:12): The references to brothers and sisters in relationship to Jesus Christ (cf. Mark 6:3; John 7:2–10) have been given three interpretations. Traditional Catholic commentators, who propose the doctrine of the perpetual virginity of Mary, believe that these references indicate either Jesus' cousins or Joseph's children by a previous marriage. Protestant commentators generally accept the view that these references describe the younger children born to Mary and Joseph. Perhaps the best attitude to take on this matter is historian Paul Maier's, that is, that, although theologians may debate the issue, most of Christianity can go along quite well with either interpretation. The New Testament tends to generalize regarding points that are not central to faith.[2]

The Passover has its roots in the Old Testament. The celebration is connected with one of the most important events in Israel's history—the Exodus of the Hebrews from slavery in Egypt. Read about the establishing of the Passover in Exodus 12, then record what you learn below. If you can, you may want to consult a Bible dictionary or encyclopedia as well.

Associated with the Passover was the annual temple offering (Ex. 30:13–16), both of which took place in Jerusalem. Pilgrims traveling to Jerusalem for these religious events had to exchange their Roman money for the Jewish half-shekel. Because Jews were required by law to spend a tenth of their income in Jerusalem (Deut. 14:23–27), citizens of Jerusalem quite willingly filled the visitors needs.[3] This included selling to worshipers—at a healthy profit, of course—the animals they would need for their sacrifices (John 2:14).

How did Jesus respond to this religious enterprise? (John 2:15)

Why did He react this way? (vv. 16, 17)

As you might imagine, the Jewish merchants and religious authorities must have been incensed by Jesus' behavior. What happened between them after Jesus drove the money changers and animals out of the temple area? (vv. 18–21)

What effect did this incident have on Jesus' disciples? (vv. 17, 22; cf. 1:11)

Do you think anyone expected Jesus to act this way? Support your answer from the text.

REBORN TO LIVE FOREVER

After cleansing the temple, Jesus stayed in Jerusalem to celebrate the Passover feast. He also performed a number of miraculous signs that led many more people to believe "in His name" (John 2:23). But verses 24 and 25 indicate that Jesus didn't respond to their faith profession as He had to His disciples'. Why? (cf. 6:2, 14, 15, 60–66)

On the heels of all these events comes Nicodemus, a Pharisee (see pp. 31, 32) and "a ruler of the Jews" (3:1), who wants to meet with Jesus while He's still in Jerusalem. As "a ruler of the Jews," Nicodemus was a member of the Sanhedrin—a ruling body of seventy-one scribes, elders, and priests. These men preserved and interpreted the law and were empowered to excommunicate persons who violated Jewish religious law and to try cases against false prophets and rebellious elders.[4]

When did Nicodemus go to meet Jesus? (3:2)

Why do you think he chose this time of day for a meeting?

What did Nicodemus say to Jesus when he first met Him; and what is its significance, especially given who Nicodemus was and the religious body he represented? (v. 2)

Do you think Nicodemus was sincere in his initial comments? Why or why not?

Before Nicodemus even asks Jesus a question, Jesus begins to speak authoritatively to him, this "ruler of the Jews." Put in your own words what Jesus tells him (vv. 3, 5–8, 10–21). Let your rewording explain rather than repeat Jesus' word choice.

  WORD WEALTH

Born again (3:3): Reborn, literally, "born *from above*"; a spiritual regeneration and transformation that takes a person out of the kingdom of darkness and death and into the kingdom of light and life, also known as the kingdom of God.[5]

Teacher of Israel (3:10): This could indicate that Nicodemus held an official teaching office in Israel. It at least means that he was a very prominent teacher, which is all the more reason, as Jesus says, that he should have understood the Hebrew Scriptures' implicit teaching regarding spiritual rebirth and its necessity for entrance into God's kingdom. The prophets alluded to this (cf. Ezek. 36:22–27; 37:1–14), and many Old Testament stories illustrated it: "The safe passage of Noah and his family through the flood, to start life anew in a new world (Gen. 6:13—9:19), the redeemed Israelites' crossing the sea of reed to be a people set apart for God (Ex. 14:15—15:21), Naaman the Syrian's 'baptism' in Jordan, whereby 'his flesh was restored like the flesh of a little child, and he was clean' (2 Kin. 5:14)."[6]

Son of Man (3:13): Emphasizes Jesus' humanity but also His heavenly origin and kingly status (cf. Ezek. 1:26–28; Dan. 7:13, 14).

Believes (3:15): Trusts, places faith in. This act involves a knowledge of, reliance upon, and a commitment to Jesus as the divine Messiah.[7]

Perish (3:15): In contrast to everlasting life, this is everlasting death or destruction (cf. Matt. 8:12; Rom. 6:23; Jude 13), which is so horrible an option that we should readily become as radical as necessary in order to avoid it (Mark 9:43–47).

Eternal life (3:15): A new order and dimension of life bestowed from above. Although it ultimately pertains to the "forever" life believers will experience in heaven, it is "abundantly" present now (John 10:10), as well as being a reality that has no end (John 5:24; 10:28).

Loved (3:16): The English translation of the Greek word *agape*, which means "unconditional, sacrificial, limitless love" (cf. Rom. 5:8; 1 Cor. 13).

Condemned (3:18): Judged, damned. The ultimate, self-imposed consequence of refusing God's love-gift.

Now go back and consider how Nicodemus responded to Jesus' teaching (3:4, 9). In light of his opening remarks to Jesus (v. 2), do you think he was prepared for what Jesus had to say? Though the apostle John doesn't tell us here, do you think Nicodemus finally understood what Jesus told him? (cf. 7:45–52; 19:38, 39)

 FAITH ALIVE

Do you understand what it means to be born again from above? Have you placed your trust in Christ and experienced the new birth, the regeneration and transformation brought about by the work of the Holy Spirit? If not, take the opportunity to do that right now, then record the date and fact of your commitment below.

On the other hand, if you know you have become and are now a child of God's kingdom, record here how you know that's so. It's often helpful, particularly when doubts come, to have a written record of our commitment to the King.

WHEN DECREASING INCREASES

Another group Jesus surprised was John the Baptist's followers. With John's blessing, some of his disciples had left him to follow Jesus (1:35–37). And although the Messiah had now arrived and had begun His ministry, John knew his ministry days were not yet over (3:24), so he continued to baptize and preach his message of repentance (v. 23). His followers seemed content with that until Jesus and His disciples began baptizing (v. 22). John's followers saw this as a threat, and they apparently got into an argument over it with some of the Jewish onlookers (v. 25). Whose baptism was the best? Which one's ministry really accorded with the Jewish understanding of purification? John's disciples wanted their master to stand up for his rights, so they went to tell him about what Jesus and His followers were doing (v. 26).

What was John's basic message to them? (vv. 27–36)

How did his understanding of Jesus' identity and mission fit with what Jesus said about Himself and His purpose?

PREPARING FOR THE UNEXPECTED

As you worked through this lesson, did Jesus ever surprise you? Do you understand why He shocked so many people? Of course, we have just begun to see the "Master of the Unexpected" at work in the Fourth Gospel. Much more is to come. In fact, in the next chapter, we'll see Jesus go head-to-head with racism, sexual immorality, religious intolerance, rejection, and a fatal disease. When you deal with Jesus, you have to prepare for the unexpected. What else could we expect from the God-man?

PROBING THE DEPTHS

The miracle of Jesus' turning water into wine almost always raises the issue of whether it's right for Christians to drink alcohol. Some believers think that the Bible teaches (explicitly or implicitly) total abstinence, while others believe that Scripture permits moderate, though not excessive, drinking. Those Christians who accept the latter view are divided, however, with some believing that abstinence is more socially responsible in a culture where alcohol abuse is a serious problem.

In case you would like to explore this issue and resolve it for yourself, I have compiled the relevant Bible texts and categorized them for easier reference. I have also provided you with a short bibliography made up of articles and books that present the various positions and defend differing viewpoints. Here you have what you need to probe the depths of the question, To drink or not to drink—what's the biblical position?

WHAT THE BIBLE SAYS

- ALCOHOL'S USE: Gen. 14:18; 27:28; Ex. 22:29; 29:38–41; Num. 15:6–10; 28:11–15; Deut. 14:26; Ruth 2:14; 1 Sam. 25:18–38; 2 Sam. 16:1, 2; Neh. 5:18; Ps. 104:14, 15; Prov. 9:4–6; 25:20; 31:6, 7; Eccl. 2:24; 9:7; Song 5:1; Is. 25:6; 55:1, 2; Joel 2:23, 24; 3:17, 18; Amos 9:13; Matt. 11:19; 26:27–29; 27:48; Mark 2:14–17, 22; 14:23–25; Luke 5:27–39; 7:34; 10:33, 34; 22:17, 18, 20; John 2:3–11; 1 Cor. 11:23–26; 1 Tim. 5:23.

- ALCOHOL'S ABUSE: Gen. 9:20–24; 19:30–38; Deut. 21:20, 21; 1 Sam. 1:13–16; Job 12:25; Prov. 20:1; 21:17; 23:17–21, 29–35; 31:4, 5; Is. 5:11, 22; 19:14; 28:7, 8; 56:12; Jer. 25:27–29; 48:26; 51:39, 40; Hos. 4:11; 7:5; Joel 1:5; Amos 6:1, 6; Hab. 2:5, 15, 16; Luke 21:34; Rom. 13:13; 1 Cor. 5:11; 6:9, 10; 11:20, 21, 27–32; Gal. 5:19–21; Eph. 5:18; 1 Tim. 3:2, 3, 8; Titus 1:7; 2:3; 1 Pet. 4:3.

- ALCOHOL RESTRICTIONS: Lev. 10:8–11; Num. 6:1–4, 13–20; Deut. 29:5, 6; Judg. 13:3–5, 7, 13, 14; Jer. 35; Ezek. 44:15, 21; Dan. 1:8–16; Matt. 11:18; Luke 1:13–15; 7:33; Eph. 5:18; 1 Tim. 3:2, 3, 8; Titus 1:7; 2:3.
- RELATED PRINCIPLES: Rom. 14; 1 Cor. 6:12; 8; 10:31; Gal. 5:22, 23; Phil. 2:3, 4; 1 Tim. 4:1–5; 6:17; Titus 1:15; 2 Pet. 1:5–11.

WHAT OTHERS SAY

Brown, C. "Vine, Wine." In *The New International Dictionary of New Testament Theology.* 4 vols. Ed. Colin Brown. Grand Rapids, MI: Zondervan Publishing House, 1978. 3:918–923.

Geisler, Norman L. *To Drink or Not to Drink? A Sober Look at the Problem.* Dallas, TX: Quest Publications, 1984.

Nelson's Illustrated Bible Dictionary. Gen. ed. Herbert Lockyer, Sr. Nashville, TN: Thomas Nelson Publishers, 1986. "Wine," 1101–1102.

Unger, Merrill F. "Drink, Strong"; "Wine." *The New Unger's Bible Dictionary.* Ed. R. K. Harrison. Chicago, IL: Moody Press, 1988. 324; 1366–1368.

Pierard, R. V. "Alcohol, Drinking of." In *Evangelical Dictionary of Theology.* Ed. Walter A. Elwell. Grand Rapids, MI: Baker Book House, 1984. 27–29.

Schultz, A. C. "Wine and Strong Drink." In *The Zondervan Pictorial Encyclopedia of the Bible.* 5 vols. Gen. ed. Merrill C. Tenney. Grand Rapids, MI: Zondervan Publishing House, 1976. 5:935–938.

Stein, Robert H. "Wine-Drinking in New Testament Times." *Christianity Today* (June 20, 1975):9–10.

1. J. Carl Laney, *John,* Moody Gospel Commentary, gen. ed. Paul Enns (Chicago, IL: Moody Press, 1992), 62.

2. Paul L. Maier, *In the Fullness of Time: A Historian Looks at Christmas, Easter, and the Early Church* (San Francisco, CA: HarperCollins, 1991), 81.

3. Laney, *John,* 70.

4. Ibid., 75, 76.

5. Edwin A. Blum, "John," in *The Bible Knowledge Commentary: New Testament Edition,* gen. eds. John F. Walvoord and Roy B. Zuck (Wheaton, IL: Victor Books, 1983), 281.

6. Taken from *The Gospel of John,* by F. F. Bruce (Grand Rapids, MI: William B. Eerdmans Publishing Company, 1983), 86. Used by permission.

7. Laney, *John,* 82.

Lesson 5/The Ultimate Thirst Quencher (4:1–54)

Have you ever stopped to think about the variety of things available for us to drink? Take juices, for example. Orange, grape, apple, pineapple, cranapple, lemon—name your fruit, and you can have it as a juice drink. Or what about soft drinks? With caffeine, without caffeine; clear or dark; with 10 percent real fruit juice or just chemicals; with sugar or sugar-free. Then you have your tea and coffee and milk options, not to mention all the alcoholic drink combinations available. Even water comes mountain fresh or polluted, with chloride or fluoride, in bottles or out of the tap, or in an endless variety of mineral water preparations. Our drinking options are enormous.

With so much available to us, you'd think we'd never get thirsty. But we do. Do we ever! Our parched palates support billion-dollar industries dedicated to keeping our unquenchable thirsts quenched.

"So what does this trivia lesson have to do with the Fourth Gospel?" I'm getting to that. The parallel is this: What's true about our insatiable physical thirst is also true about our spiritual thirst—that parched ground within us all, longing to be drenched with the never-ending waters of ultimate purpose, meaning, forgiveness, redemption, renewal. Here, too, our options are enormous. We can drink at the fountain of ancient religions, such as Islam, Judaism, Buddhism, Hinduism, Zoroastrianism, or Confucianism. Or, if our tastes turn to more contemporary structures of ancient error, we might sample Mormonism, Jehovah's Witnesses, Christian Science, the Baha'i faith, or the latest reincarnationist or New Age guru. And these are just a few of the hundreds of options, all claiming to have the ability to satisfy our dry, cracking souls.

Where can we find the thirst quencher we really need? Who has the answer? John the apostle does, and it's embedded in the fourth chapter of the gospel that bears his name. Here we'll learn about a drink that has no equal. Once you taste it, once you let it touch the tongue of your soul, it will flood your entire being until you stand fully soaked for an eternity.

So get ready to throw out any other so-called spiritual drinks you may have been tasting. You can also toss any other kinds of drinks you've tried to quench the dry ache within. You're about to find out about the ultimate thirst-quencher— the only drink that never needs replenishing, the only one that can satisfy your soul forever.

THE FOUNTAIN OF ETERNAL LIFE

While Jesus and His disciples were carrying on a baptism ministry in Judea, Jesus learned that the Pharisees had gotten wind of the fact that His ministry was baptizing more people than John the Baptist's was. So this led Jesus to pull up stakes, pack His tent, and start off for Galilee (John 4:1–3).

Why would Jesus move His ministry site because the Pharisees discovered how successful He was? Was He afraid of them, or did He have a different motivation? (cf. 7:6–8, 30; 8:20)

      WORD WEALTH

Lord (4:1): A form of address to a respected person, similar to our word *sir* (v. 11; 9:36). It can also signify Jesus' deity (20:28).

FAITH ALIVE

Several times throughout this study, we'll see Jesus leaving a place or a group at just the right time. He always seemed to know when it was time to move on. How do you think He knew?

How can you know when it's time? List some ways God lets us know.

Has He been telling you lately to move on? to stay? Have you been listening? If not, why? If so, how is the transition going? Share your thoughts with the Lord. He's always willing to listen and guide a responsive mind and heart.

Now Judea was southern Palestine, the region in which Jerusalem resided, and Galilee was in the northernmost section of Palestine. Directly between Judea and Galilee lay Samaria. To the east was the region of Perea. When Jews wanted to go from Judea to Galilee, they often went northeast through Perea, then crossed west into Galilee, even though the Samaria route was much shorter. Why would they avoid Samaria? (4:9)

BEHIND THE SCENES

You can't understand the antagonism that existed between first-century Jews and Samaritans without knowing some history.

God had chosen Jerusalem as the worship center for Israel. It was built on Mt. Moriah where Abraham had offered Isaac (Gen. 22:2), and it was the site where the temple had finally been built by Solomon (2 Chr. 3:1, 2). Jerusalem was definitely the holy city (6:6; 12:13; Jer. 3:17; Zech. 14:16).

But when Israel split into two kingdoms (931 B.C.), the ruler of the northern kingdom, Jeroboam, wanted to ensure that the people in his domain didn't shift their allegiance to Rehoboam, the ruler of the southern kingdom (Judah), after traveling to Jerusalem to worship (1 Kin. 12:27). So Jeroboam established golden-calf worship centers in the North and instituted a substitute feast for Jerusalem's Passover, which continued until the northern kingdom fell to the Assyrians in 722 B.C.

The Assyrians forced most of the Israelites to leave and replaced them with foreigners from Mesopotamia, who brought their own foreign gods and customs and syncretized them with the remaining Israelites' worship of the true God (2 Kin. 17:24–41). It was out of this idolatrous hybrid that first-century Samaria grew its religious beliefs and practices.

When the exiled Israelites began returning to their homeland (539 B.C.), they were appalled with the compromises the Samaritans had made with the foreign settlers, so the returning Jews would not allow the Samaritans to participate in the rebuilding of the temple in Jerusalem (Ezra 4:1–3). This exacerbated the division between the two groups (vv. 4, 5; Neh. 4:1, 2) and eventually led to the Samaritans' building their own temple on Mt. Gerizim in Samaria, which was later burned by the Jewish leader John Hyrcanus in 128 B.C.

Jews took pains to avoid contact with Samaritans and looked on them as unclean. Now you can see why they hated each other.

Jesus had a choice of routes. He could avoid hated Samaria and travel to Galilee via Perea, or He could take His chances and pass through Samaria. He made the latter choice (John 4:4). Why?

Where did Jesus arrive in Samaria and what is its significance? (vv. 5, 6; cf. Gen. 33:18–20)

WORD WEALTH

Sychar (John 4:5): This village was just inside the southern section of Samaria, and it lay between Mt. Ebal and Mt. Gerizim.

Sixth hour (4:6): If Jewish reckoning is used, the sixth hour was noon. According to Roman time reckoning, it would have been 6:00 P.M.

What resting spot did Jesus pick, and whom did He meet there? (vv. 6, 7)

What request did He make, and what was the response? (vv. 7, 9)

BEHIND THE SCENES

In first-century Jewish culture, as in most of the world, women were not held in appropriate esteem. Samaritan women, as far as Jewish prejudice was concerned, were even farther down the acceptability scale for two reasons. First, they were Samaritans, and second, they were considered to be unclean. To drink from a Samaritan woman's vessel resulted in one's becoming ceremonially unclean. Jesus ignored these perceptions and thereby challenged the racial and religious bigotry He faced, for the Samaritans were equally biased against Jews.

The next exchange between the Samaritan woman and Jesus gets to the heart of what He offers her (vv. 10–14). What is His offer?

Does she understand what He's talking about? (vv. 11, 12, 15)

What does Jesus do to get her attention, and what conclusion does she begin to draw about Him? (vv. 16–19)

Why do you think she then shifts the discussion to where one should worship—whether on Mt. Gerizim or in Jerusalem? (v. 20)

Does Jesus take the bait and enter into the debate over the right place to worship? What *does* He say about worship? (vv. 21–24)

Notice how the Samaritan woman responds to Jesus' teaching on worship (v. 25). Was she shifting the subject again? expressing her longings? trying to put Jesus in His place by appealing to someone she thought would have more knowledge and authority than He? What do you think?

What does Jesus proclaim to the Samaritan woman, and how does she respond to the revelation? (John 4:26, 28, 29)

What happens in Samaria as a result of her testimony? (vv. 30, 39–42)

WORD WEALTH

Savior (4:42): Deliverer, rescuer, preserver.

FARMERS DESPERATELY NEEDED

You probably noticed that before Jesus ever met this woman, while He was just sitting beside the well trying to recover from His long day of travel, His disciples had "gone away into the city to buy food" (v. 8). Then just as Jesus declares His messiahship to her, the disciples return and find Him talking to her. They are so stunned they can't talk, which gives the woman a chance to leave before any kind of confrontation can occur (vv. 27, 28). Still trying to ignore the taboos Jesus had violated, the disciples finally offer Him some of the food they had brought back with them (v. 31). But Jesus won't let them off the hook. What does He say to them? (vv. 32–38)

As Jesus spoke to them, what would the disciples have seen coming toward them? (vv. 30, 35)

Given the great animosity between Jews and Samaritans, how do you think the disciples must have felt as they were surrounded by their enemies and told to minister to them?

FAITH ALIVE

There was no room in Jesus' life for prejudice, bigotry, hatred—anything that would keep Him from reaching out to others with His Father's gift of salvation. Jesus wouldn't allow any of these factors to hamper His disciples either.

How about you? Are you holding back on ministry opportunities, relationships, travel plans, whatever, because of prejudice? bigotry? hatred? some sort of rivalry? any other reason inappropriate for God's disciples? Deal with that here, now, before the Lord of the harvest. He has so much to accomplish, and He wants you to join Him and reap the benefits. Don't let these cages lock you in and keep you from all God has for you and wants to do through you. Ask the Holy Spirit to unveil unperceived areas of prejudice or racism, resentment or insensitivity to others.

AN UNSURE WELCOME

After an incredible two days of ministry in Samaria, Jesus hits the road again and finally arrives in Galilee.

How do the Galileans respond to His visit and why? (v. 45; cf. 2:13–25)

Did Jesus always receive this kind of welcome in His home region? (v. 44; cf. Mark 6:4–6; Luke 4:24–28) What happened on some of those occasions?

FROM A DISTANCE

While in Galilee, Jesus returns to Cana, "where He had made the water wine" (John 4:46).

Who comes to Him there? (v. 46)

Where is he from, and what does he want? (vv. 46, 47)

How does Jesus deal with the man's cry for help? (vv. 48–50)

Do you think Jesus treated him roughly? Why or why not?

What does the man do in response, and what does he discover after he leaves Jesus behind? (vv. 49, 50–53)

What happens next? (v. 53)

Why does the apostle John record this event? (v. 54)

Lesson 6/Like Father, Like Son (5:1–47)

God created us in His image. The Bible is clear on that (Gen. 1:27; 9:6; James 3:9). What this means is that we *resemble* and *represent* our Creator. Like Him we can think, feel, choose, act, refrain, develop relationships, love, and create. In these ways we resemble Him. We represent Him in many ways, too. He has given us stewardship over the earth, the authority to enter into covenants with each other, as well as with Him, the responsibilities to execute justice, rule, and serve, and the privilege to be ambassadors to the world, spreading the gospel of Christ by the power of His Holy Spirit and making disciples.

Like our Creator, one of the greatest powers we have is the power to create. We can bring into existence paintings, music, theories, buildings, furniture, factories, concepts, cars, trains, planes, clothes, produce—all kinds of ideas and goods meant to benefit human beings in some way. But we can also create something more intimate, more valuable, indeed, of eternal value: other human beings. In our own image, we produce sons and daughters (Gen. 5:1–3), give them names, food, and clothes, and educate them, and set them on their own to repeat the process. They, too, resemble and represent us. They look like us, sound like us, think like us, even feel like us. They also carry on our values, perspectives, and names. When others see them, they believe our children stand for who we are and what we've done. Sometimes our children make us feel proud; at other times we wish we could fire them and hire replacements.

Our heavenly Father has a Son—an eternal, uncreated Son, but a Son who is just like Him. His Son resembles and represents Him with utter perfection, so the Father is always pleased with Him. Consequently, when we see Jesus, His Son, we can see the Father shining through.

So let's look more closely at Jesus. He'll show us the Father we can't see or touch.

DO YOU WANT TO BE HEALED?

John 5 opens with Jesus in Jerusalem to attend an un-named Jewish feast (v. 1). Where does Jesus turn up there, and what happens? (vv. 2–9)

 WORD WEALTH

Sheep Gate (5:2): One of the entryways in the wall that surrounded Jerusalem. This opening was in the north wall of the city (cf. Neh. 3:1, 32; 12:39).[1]

Bethesda (5:2): "Place of Outpouring" or "House of Grace."[2] The pool of Bethesda was actually twin pools large enough to swim in. They may have been filled partly from the great reservoirs of Solomon's Pools (which were southwest of Bethlehem) and partly from an intermittent spring that periodically stirred up the water.[3]

 BEHIND THE SCENES

The words "waiting for the moving of the water" (v. 3) to the end of verse 4 are absent from all extant copies of John's gospel until A.D. 400. For this reason many Bible scholars see this section of John 5 as a copyist's explanatory insertion, not as part of the original, God-inspired text. However, the rest of the narrative makes clear that there was nonetheless an unusual presence at work there on occasion (v. 7). Although such copying insertions have occurred over the years during the transmission of the Scriptures, they are innocent of dis-honest intent (as with this explanatory phrase), and none of them affects any key issue of Christian doctrine.

BIBLE EXTRA

For more about how the Scriptures were transmitted over the centuries, including how scholars can tell what material was part of the original text, you may find the following sources helpful: *A General Introduction to the Bible,* by Norman L. Geisler and William E. Nix, rev. ed. (Chicago, IL: Moody Press, 1986); *From Ancient Tablets to Modern Translations: A General Introduction to the Bible,* by David Ewert (Grand Rapids, MI: Zondervan Publishing House, 1983).

Out of all the hurting people seeking to get well around the pool of Bethesda, why do you think Jesus chose only one person to heal?

Why would Jesus ask the lame man if he wanted to get well? (vv. 6, 7) Was His question cruel or superfluous?

How did Jesus heal this man, and how long did it take the paralytic to experience healing and renewed strength? (vv. 8, 9)

WORD WEALTH

Bed (5:8): A straw mat that could be rolled up and carried on the shoulder.[4]

The Jews (5:10): Throughout John's gospel, this refers essentially to those religious leaders who sustained an antagonistic posture against Jesus and His ministry. It is not referring to the general Jewish public of that or any other particular time and should not be read as containing a social or ethnic bias. It relates to an internal struggle relevant to the times of the text.

On what day did Jesus heal this man, and what problem did that raise? (vv. 9–16)

What did Jesus do after He performed the healing? (vv. 13–15) Why?

What does verse 14 mean? Does it suggest the source of this man's former paralytic condition? Does it refer to his response to Jesus or the Jews? Or does it indicate something else?

It appears that the healed man betrayed Jesus (vv. 12, 13, 15). Do you think so? Why or why not?

 **FAITH ALIVE**

What can we expect of God's healing power today? Support your answer from Scripture.

Have you known someone who was supernaturally healed as the paralytic was? If so, record what happened; then stop to give praise to the Lord for His healing promises and fulfillment.

Have you had an instance when a loved one was not healed? What happened? How did you feel about it? Were you disappointed, frustrated, or angry toward God? Are you still? Be honest with your feelings and share them with the Lord. He can handle them.

LORD, LIAR, OR LUNATIC?

Jesus was never one to back down, especially when He wanted to make a point that His audience desperately needed to hear and understand. So, in the face of a lynch-mob mentality, Jesus laid out some of the most direct and challenging teaching the people had heard from Him so far.

Put in your own words Jesus' response to the charge His Jewish critics made against Him (vv. 16, 17).

What response did Jesus' answer provoke? (v. 18)

Do you think His critics correctly understood Jesus' answer? Why or why not?

From John 5:19–47, Jesus answers the charge that He claimed to be "equal with God" (v. 18). He gives the Jews several reasons to accept His claim to deity. Outline His answer below, restating each of His reasons and the support He gives for each. Here Jesus tells us how He is like His Father.

JESUS' CASE FOR DIVINE EQUALITY

HIS REASONS	HIS EVIDENCE

In His lengthy answer, Jesus mentioned that people could make positive or negative responses to His claims, and, along with their responses, would come the appropriate consequences. Summarize the responses and their consequences below.

The Negatives (vv. 23, 28, 29, 38–47):

The Positives (vv. 24, 25, 28, 29):

Why did Jesus spend more time focusing on the negatives?

Why did He take this opportunity to defend His equality with the Father? (v. 34)

1. F. F. Bruce, *The Gospel of John* (Grand Rapids, MI: William B. Eerdmans Publishing Company, 1983), 122.

2. *Spirit-Filled Life Bible* (Nashville, TN: Thomas Nelson Publishers, 1991), 1581, note on 5:2.

3. Bruce, *The Gospel of John*, 122.

4. Ibid., 124.

Lesson 7/Great Signs, Hard Sayings
(6:1–71)

- Great moral teacher
- Peace advocate
- Prophet
- King without a country
- Civil rights leader
- Healer
- Rebel
- Fanatic
- Lunatic
- Magician
- Con artist
- Son of God

Jesus has been given many labels by friends and enemies alike. Hardly anyone lacks an opinion. And for good reason. History has never seen such a one as Jesus of Nazareth. From His conception in the womb of a virgin to His ascension into heaven to reign with the Father as Lord of the universe, Jesus' earthly life has raised eyebrows and voices, commissioned missionaries, created heroes and martyrs, and inspired some of the finest music, paintings, architecture, and literature the world has ever known. No other leader has had such an incredible impact on so many people for so long.

He was multifaceted and controversial. At the same time, He would be deeply loved and just as deeply hated. Sometimes His message was so clear that everyone understood what He said. At other times, however, not even His closest followers tracked with Him. His teaching was pointed, practical, and often hard to handle, and His miracles didn't always lead to high rankings in popularity contests. Jesus was a disturbing figure.

John 6 reveals this Jesus in some of His complexity. It shows Him doing great wonders, but it also shows Him presenting some troubling teaching. Friend and foe alike are seen struggling with Him, just as they do today. Truth does that to us, doesn't it? It rarely leaves us comfortable. So let's press beyond our comfort zones and discover what awaits us in the sixth chapter of John's gospel.

A LITTLE GOES A LONG WAY

The central event in John 6 is the one that opens up the chapter. Read verses 1–14 and recount the event in your own words.

The phrase "after these things" (6:1) makes a summary reference to what happened in John 5, as the writer moves rapidly past intervening events. Look into the other three gospels to see other things that occurred before John 6. Look up the following passages, and summarize what they tell us about the events leading up to the feeding of the five thousand.

Mark 6:14–29

Mark 6:7–13, 30, 31

Luke 9:7–9

What was the geographical setting for the sign in John 6:1–14? (cf. Mark 6:35; Luke 9:10)

✎ WORD WEALTH

Tiberias (v. 1): Named after the regional capital city, built on the west shore of the Sea of Galilee by Herod Antipas and named in honor of the Roman Emperor Tiberius. At the time of Jesus' ministry, this lake probably didn't have the Tiberias name yet, but it certainly did by the time John the apostle wrote his gospel.[1]

Why did such a great crowd of people follow Jesus to this place? (v. 2)

Verse 3 suggests that Jesus was trying to get away to a remote spot to be alone with His disciples. Why? The following passages will help you answer this question.

Matt. 14:1–13

Mark 6:30–33

Luke 9:1–11

What would be the significance of mentioning the Passover feast here? (John 6:4; Ex. 13:3–10; 1 Cor. 5:7, 8)

Why would Jesus use this occasion to "test" Philip when He already knew what He was going to do? (John 6:5, 6)

Did Philip, or any of the other disciples, pass the test? (vv. 7–9)

 WORD WEALTH

Test (v. 6): Try, prove, examine someone's character or faith.

Two hundred denarii (v. 7): Approximately eight months' wages for a rural laborer.[2]

 FAITH ALIVE

Has your faith and character been tested? What was the test?

How did you do through it? What did you learn about yourself and God as a result?

From the miracle Jesus performed, what did the crowd conclude about Him? (v. 14)

Did their understanding lead to appropriate action? (v. 15) Why or why not?

The gospel calls this event a "sign" (v. 14). How many signs did the apostle John record before this one, and what were they?

Why do you think that, among all the miracles Jesus performed (excluding His resurrection), this one is the only miracle recorded in all four gospels? What makes this miracle so significant?

THE WATER WALK

When Jesus left the crowd behind, "He departed again to the mountain by Himself alone" (v. 15). Why do you think He didn't take His disciples with Him? What could He have been doing?

Describe what happened after it became dark and Jesus still hadn't returned to His disciples (vv. 16–21).

 FAITH ALIVE

When you go through stormy times, like most people, you probably get scared. You may also handle your fears by drawing on your own resources. Although that's normal, too, it's not the best way to go. This biblical account suggests a better way. What is it? How can you apply it the next time you feel afraid?

LIVING BREAD

From John 6:22 to the end of the chapter, Jesus reveals a great deal about who He is, His mission, and what people can receive from Him. One of His revelations—"a hard saying"—leads to a significant drop in the numbers of His followers. He conveys these truths to a large crowd made up of four distinct groups. See if you can identify them.

Group 1 (vv. 22–26):

Group 2 (vv. 41, 59):

Group 3 (vv. 60, 66):

Group 4 (v. 67):

The first group raised four issues with Jesus. What were they, and what were Jesus' responses? (vv. 25–40) Be sure to fill in the identity of the group in the space provided in the heading just below.

JESUS' ANSWERS TO THE _____

Issue 1 (v. 25):

Jesus' response (vv. 26, 27):

Issue 2 (v. 28):

Jesus' response (v. 29):

Issue 3 (vv. 30, 31):

Jesus' response (vv. 32, 33):

Issue 4 (v. 34):

Jesus' response (vv. 35–40):

Jesus' dealings with this group raised several questions in the minds of a smaller but outspoken group. Who were they, what issues concerned them, and what answers did Jesus give them?

JESUS' ANSWERS TO THE _____

Issue 5 (vv. 41, 42):

Jesus' response (vv. 43–51):

Issue 6 (v. 52):

Jesus' response (vv. 53–58):

Once again, Jesus' answers created a problem with a third group that was much closer to Him.

JESUS' ANSWERS TO THE _____

Issue 7 (v. 60):

Jesus' response (vv. 61–65):

The group's reaction (v. 66):

In verse 67, Jesus asks a question of those who had gathered around Him. Then after the group answers, He responds with a telling question meant more to inform than to solicit an answer. Whom does He address? What does He ask/tell them? How do they (or the gospel's writer) respond to Him?

JESUS' QUESTIONS TO THE _____

Jesus' question (v. 67):

Answer 1 (vv. 68, 69):

Jesus' question (v. 70):

Answer 2 (v. 71):

Before pressing on, read back through verses 25–71, and record the "I am" sayings of Jesus—these are the words He prefaced with "I am." Then indicate what you think these sayings tell us about who Jesus is. In the Fourth Gospel, all the "I am" sayings play a very important role. We'll look at them more closely later in this study.

PROBING THE DEPTHS

Jesus' hard saying is indeed hard. His words about eating His flesh and drinking His blood have been interpreted a variety of ways by Christians throughout the centuries.

Some see His words as referring to the Eucharist, or Lord's Supper. And among those who do, four views have been held. One is called *transubstantiation*, and it's embraced by Roman Catholicism. It teaches that in a mysterious way the bread and drink of the Eucharist really become Jesus' body and blood.

A second view, *consubstantiation,* is common among Lutherans, and it says that Jesus' body and blood are present in, with, and under the Eucharistic elements of bread and wine, but they do not turn into these elements.

The third position is the *spiritual* view, which many Protestant Reformers accept. It sees Jesus' flesh-and-blood teaching as symbolic or metaphorical, indicating that through the elements of the Eucharist Christ's presence and our union with Him are manifest spiritually, not physically or materially.

The *memorial* view, which is held by many Protestants, takes Jesus' words as parallel to the Jewish Passover feast. Both meals—the Lord's Supper and the Passover—are meals of remembrance, celebrated to remind believers of what God has done to save them and to participate by faith in the present power of the covenant relationship represented in the rite.

A fifth position, held by some Catholics as well as Protestants, could be called the *way-to-salvation* view. It proposes that Jesus' words about eating His flesh and drinking His blood are parallel to and carry the same meaning as seeing and believing in Him in order to receive eternal life (John 6:40). Consequently, from this viewpoint, Jesus' words in John 6 have nothing to do with the Lord's Supper; they are merely another way of telling people how they can be saved.

Interpretations vary, but given the weight Jesus placed on these words, we should settle the matter with spiritual discernment and sensitivity, emphasizing the spiritual meaning, as Jesus said (v. 63).

Many readers may be helped to a nondivisive, contemporarily dynamic approach to the Lord's Table by Jack Hayford's book *Worship His Majesty.*

1. F. F. Bruce, *The Gospel of John* (Grand Rapids, MI: William B. Eerdmans Publishing Company, 1983), 142.
2. J. Carl Laney, *John*, Moody Gospel Commentary, gen. ed. Paul Enns (Chicago, IL: Moody Press, 1992), 121, 122.

Lesson 8/*On the Defense*
(7:1—8:59)

There once was an author who created a whole world in his mind. The landscape, colors, smells, sights . . . everything about this world had his fingerprints. Even its creatures, great and small, reflected him in some way.

One day, while he was writing the story about this world, he decided to make himself part of the story, so he wrote himself into it, making himself like one of the higher creatures. He thought his world would welcome him joyfully, since he was the one who gave it life in the first place. So he arrived with high expectations.

Once inside his world, he decided to remain inconspicuous for awhile, so he could observe it firsthand. Some of what he saw greatly pleased him. The trees, animals, sea life, sky, and other aspects of the natural world were even more beautiful and harmonious to his eyes than his words had described. Here he had done well. On the other hand, the higher creatures he had made—those he called the freethinkers—were having trouble getting along with each other and their surroundings. In fact, they disagreed with one another far more than there were issues to dispute over. This upset the author, so he decided to do something about it.

Picking just the right moment, he introduced himself to a prestigious gathering of the Freethinkers High Society. He told them that he was their author, their creator, and that he would be delighted to help them resolve their differences. "You've got to be kidding!" they told him. "Who do you think you are?"

"I told you," he said. "I gave birth to you. At one time you were just a part of my imagination. But I gave you life. I put pen to paper and brought you into being. Now I would like to create some solutions for you."

With incredulity written all over their faces, they replied, "You must be nuts! You look like one of us, you sound like one of us, but you're certainly not as intelligent as we are, otherwise, you wouldn't be talking such nonsense."

"Oh, but I assure you I am who I say I am," the author said. But no matter what proof he provided, only a few of the Freethinkers would believe him, and those were ostracized from the Freethinkers High Society. The author's world had rejected him and his defense.

Jesus' situation was not unlike this author's. He, too, created a world with the wisdom within His own mind, and He knew it was good. But when some of His creatures went wrong, He worked to steer them in the right direction. Eventually, He even came to the earth in the form of a man so those of His free creatures who had gone wrong could better see and hear Him. But they turned on Him. Except for a few, His free creatures not only rejected His counsel but Him as well. They would not believe that He was their Creator, regardless of the evidence He offered.

In John 7 and 8, this truth comes through with painful clarity. Here the Son of God presents proof after proof of His identity, but those who say they are God's people keep rejecting His Son's defense. Willfully ignorant? Yes. Tragic? Without a doubt. Still going on today? Sadly, yes. Could it be happening with you or someone you love? As you work through this chapter of our study, you be the judge.

THE HEAT INCREASES

Up until this point in John's gospel, Jesus has gotten mixed reviews among the populace and the religious authorities. For the moment, imagine that you are a movie critic and that Jesus is the star performer in a new release about His life story. You desire to report, not what you think about His performance and His movie, but what others are saying about it. So you spend several days interviewing many people who have seen the show and talked with Jesus. From your reading of John 1—6, what would you say in your review? Write it here as you might report it.

From John 7 on, whatever polarization you noticed in earlier chapters increases considerably. The following verses will give you some indication of how hot things become. Like a good reporter, objectively summarize what you discover.

7:1

7:5

7:10–13

7:20

7:25–27

7:30, 31

7:32

7:40–44

7:45–52

8:3–6

8:13

8:20

8:30

8:41–44

8:48

8:52, 53

8:59

What's your overall assessment? Based only on the audience's response to Jesus, would you give Him and His "show" a thumbs-up or a thumbs-down?

Explain your answer.

Now let's get a more detailed perspective of John 7 and 8.

FAMILY DISBELIEF

John 7 opens with the Son of God, Jesus Christ, avoiding a section of real estate that is rightfully His as Creator. What section of Palestine is He avoiding and why? (v. 1)

The events recorded in John 7 and 8 surround a Jewish religious festival called the Feast of Tabernacles (7:2), or the Festival of Booths, or the Feast of Ingathering. For some important background about this celebration, see Exodus 23:14–16; Leviticus 23:33–36, 39–43; Numbers 29:12–38; Deuteronomy 16:13–17.

On the occasion of such an incredible religious festival, some family members come to Jesus and scoff at Him. What do they challenge Him to do? (John 7:3–5)

Why won't Jesus comply? (vv. 6–8)

 FAITH ALIVE

Jesus was so confident of the Father's will for Him that He could stand firm in the face of the challenges from unbelievers, even when those challenges came from loved ones. How about you? Are you spending sufficient time with the Lord, seeking His will for your life, so you can see unbelief for what it is, regardless of its source? Are you able to stand up to challenges meant to snub your faith? Take these matters to the Lord in prayer. Feel free to journal your thoughts or even your prayer in the space provided here. He's waiting to hear from you.

Perhaps you have unbelieving family members who do not understand your faith and even ridicule it. Jesus knows your pain. He had loved ones, too, who treated His convictions with disdain.

Acknowledge your hurt before Him. He longs to comfort you. Remember the promise of God's Word, also (Acts 16:31), and remain patient and steadfast in praise-filled prayer.

A SECRET TOO BIG TO HIDE

So Jesus' "brothers" go to Jerusalem in Judea to attend the Feast of Tabernacles while Jesus stays behind in Galilee (John 7:9, 10). But Jesus doesn't stay in Galilee for long. In fact, He goes to the Feast, but He does so "in secret" (v. 10). Why do you think He went after all?

Although Jesus didn't draw attention to Himself when He arrived at the Feast, why was it impossible for Him to keep His presence a secret? (vv. 10–13)

What indication do you see that He never intended to stay hidden throughout the entire celebration? (v. 14)

  WORD WEALTH

The Jews (7:11, 13): Since the crowd attending the Feast of Tabernacles would have been Jewish, the phrase "the Jews" refers specifically to the Jewish religious authorities, while more generic words such as "the people" indicates the general Jewish populace.

What would be the possible significance of Jesus' exposing His presence in Jerusalem's temple? (v. 14)

THE FIRST REACTIONS AND CHARGES

With the secret out and Jesus teaching in the temple, we get the first glimpses of how the populace and religious authorities respond to Him at the Feast. What was the initial response of the religious authorities to Jesus' teaching? (v. 15)

BEHIND THE SCENES

Generally, aspiring students studied under leading rabbis and memorized what Jewish teachers had taught concerning the law.[1] Since Jesus hadn't been educated that way, the religious authorities couldn't figure out how He had become so learned.

How did Jesus explain the acquisition of His knowledge? (v. 16)

How could others verify His claims? (vv. 17, 18)

What made Him so special? (vv. 18, 19)

The people didn't like Jesus' answer so they charged Him with being demon-possessed (v. 20). What was His defense against this charge? (vv. 21–24)

FAITH ALIVE

Have you ever judged "according to appearance" rather than "with righteous judgment"? (v. 24) What happened and what did you learn from it?

Have you misjudged again recently? If so, have you set things right with that person and the Lord? Reconciliation is very important to God, so it should also be to us (Matt. 5:23–26). Plan now when and how you will seek to restore the relationship.

Summarize the exchange that followed between the people and Jesus:

The people's rebuttal (vv. 25–27):

Jesus' answer (vv. 28, 29):

The mixed response (vv. 30, 31):

WORD WEALTH

Cried out (v. 28): Expressed loudly with strong emotion, often associated with making a solemn pronouncement (cf. 1:15; 7:37; 12:44).[2]

THE TEMPERATURE RISES

If things hadn't gotten hot enough, they quickly increased. People were turning to Jesus, which the religious authorities saw as a definite threat. So the Pharisees and chief priests "sent officers to take [arrest] Him" (7:32). Interpret Jesus' response to them (vv. 33, 34).

What did the religious leaders think He meant? (vv. 35, 36)

WORD WEALTH

The Dispersion (7:35): "Refers to Jews scattered throughout the Greek world. Later the term also denoted the Christians scattered abroad (1 Pet. 1:1)."[3]

The Greeks (7:35): Non-Jewish or pagan peoples of that society, not only natives of Greece or Greek-speaking people.

BEHIND THE SCENES

"Each day during the Feast of Tabernacles a joyous celebration was observed in which the priests brought water (symbolic of the water supplied from the rock in Ex. 17) to the temple from the pool of Siloam in a golden pitcher. During the procession the people recited Is. 12:3. The water was poured out on the altar as an offering to God, while the people shouted and sang. Jesus was the fulfillment of all that the ceremony typified (see 1 Cor. 10:4)."[4]

On the last day of the Feast, Jesus spoke to the crowd again. What did He say, and what does it mean? (vv. 37–39)

What event is Jesus prophesying, since this text points to a time after His death, resurrection, and ascension? When do you think His prophesied "rivers of living water" were poured out? Might we appropriately compare this text with Acts 2:1–39?

Jesus also uses the image of "water" in John 4. Draw a comparison on your own, noting the difference between the "well" or "spring" that supplies an individual's own personal thirst and the "rivers" that flow outward from a Holy Spirit-filled person in serving and ministering to others.

 FAITH ALIVE

To your viewpoint, are there any implications in this comparison of texts for the need of being both satisfied in knowing Christ and also filled with the Spirit and overflowing Christ. Write your feelings of response to these thoughts.

What was the crowd's response to Jesus' words? (John 7:40–44)

AUTHORITATIVE CONFUSION

The plot thickens in John 7:45–53. Here we get an inside look at what the religious leaders think about Jesus, and it's far from a unanimous opinion. Look over these verses, and mine their gold by answering the following questions.

Who attended the high-level meeting?

What opinions did they hold about Jesus?

What do Nicodemus's words indicate to you about his attitude toward Jesus?

A TRAP BACKFIRES

After the Feast of Tabernacles was over, the people went home, but Jesus departed to the Mount of Olives (7:53—8:1). What's the significance of this place?

Zech. 14:3, 4

Matt. 21:1–5

Matt. 24:3

Matt. 26:29, 30

Luke 19:36–40

Luke 22:39–53

In light of these passages, why do you think Jesus chose to spend the night on this mountain?

The next morning, Jesus returned to the temple to teach (John 8:2). While He was teaching, what happened and how did He handle the situation? (vv. 3–11)

 FAITH ALIVE

It's very easy to condemn someone else's sin while ignoring our own. Jesus not only rebuked that practice here, but He had strong words to say about it elsewhere as well (cf. Matt. 7:1–5).

Consider how He dealt with the adulteress and the crowd who self-righteously condemned her, and apply that to your own situation. Ask the Lord to help you see your situation clearly; then be open to what He reveals to you and be sensitive to how He wants you to handle it. Mercy and grace await you if you will just be vulnerable before Him.

THE DEFENSE ALMOST RESTS—PERMANENTLY

From John 8:12 to the end of the chapter, Jesus offers a defense against a number of charges, misunderstandings, and questions, all of which we'll call *claims.* Summarize the claims made against Him, His responses, the people's actions, and the Lord's. Then render your verdict: Did Jesus make His case or not?

Jesus' first statement (v. 12):

Claim 1 (v. 13):

Jesus' answer (vv. 14–18):

Claim 2 (v. 19):

Jesus' answer (v. 19):

Jesus' second statement (v. 21):

Claim 3 (v. 22):

Jesus' answer (vv. 23, 24):

Claim 4 (v. 25):

Jesus' answer (vv. 25–29):

Jews' action (v. 30):

Jesus' third statement (vv. 31, 32):

Claim 5 (v. 33):

Jesus' answer (vv. 34–38):

Claim 6 (v. 39):

Jesus' answer (vv. 39–41)

Claim 7 (v. 41):

Jesus' answer (vv. 42–47):

Claim 8 (v. 48):

Jesus' answer (vv. 49–51):

Claim 9 (vv. 52, 53):

Jesus' answer (vv. 54–56):

Claim 10 (v. 57):

Jesus' answer (v. 58):

Jews' action (v. 59):

Jesus' action (v. 59):

Your verdict:

WORD WEALTH

Before Abraham was, I AM (8:58): Jesus is declaring that before Abraham, the father of the nation of Israel, was born, He existed eternally as God. Jesus takes the most sacred name of God as it was revealed to Moses (Ex. 3:14) and applies it to Himself. The name *YHWH* ("I AM WHO I AM") is a declaration of uncreated, eternal self-existence. Nothing can bring God into existence, and nothing can remove existence from Him. He is always. Period. Because Jesus made this claim, the Jewish authorities sought to stone Him for blasphemy.

FAITH ALIVE

From this interchange between Jesus and the religious authorities, what struck you?

What application would you draw from that?

What can you start doing about that this week? Be sure to ask the Holy Spirit to help you make your plans and implement them.

1. J. Carl Laney, *John*, Moody Gospel Commentary, gen. ed. Paul Enns (Chicago, IL: Moody Press, 1992), 141.

2. Ibid., 143; Edwin A. Blum, "John" in *The Bible Knowledge Commentary: New Testament Edition*, gen. eds. John F. Walvoord and Roy B. Zuck (Wheaton, IL: Victor Books, 1983), 300.

3. *Spirit-Filled Life Bible* (Nashville, TN: Thomas Nelson Publishers, 1991), 1587, note on 7:35.

4. Ibid., note on 7:37–39.

Lesson 9/ When the Blind See and the Seeing Are Blind (9:1—10:39)

It's an amazing thing. You can tell a young child why she shouldn't cross a busy street or touch a hot stove, and even though she signals to you that she understands, she'll do what you warned her not to do. Then, when you ask her why she did it, she'll say "I don't know" in a voice that makes you wonder if she ever understood you in the first place.

Amazingly enough, this phenomena doesn't end with adolescence. You can tell your teenage son why he should work harder in school or practice his musical instrument more often or choose better friends, and you can make your case with incredible clarity and conviction, but if he doesn't want to accept what you say, he won't. And when you ask him why he didn't follow your advice, you'll get that same babyish answer: "I don't know." Or, more sophisticated yet, "I just didn't want to." But when you ask why, you will probably still hear "I don't know."

Does adulthood cure this condition? Nope. If anything, our adulthood can advance this condition to new stages of absurdity. We become more adept at rationalizing away very good reasons and clear explanations for accepting or rejecting certain ideas, positions, or behaviors. Of course, as adults we have matured beyond "I don't know." Instead we repeat questions, giving the impression that we never heard or understood what we had been told several times already. Or, better yet, we give "reasons" for rejecting what we were told, but we have no real supporting evidence to back up our case. Or, even better, we gather a bunch of people around us who accept what we have to say; but most of them have been conned by us, so at best they know only what we do, which is in error anyway.

Why don't we just say "I don't want to do it" or "I refuse to believe that"? Why don't we just get honest about it? Many answers to these questions are possible, but the most direct is the most accurate: we often don't get honest with ourselves because our sin has blinded us to the truth. We so often cultivate a life built on denial, refusal, lies, and rationalizations that we actually lose sight of what's true. We can't see ourselves clearly anymore, so we certainly can't see others with any clarity either. We become the blind guiding the blind and too easily fall prey to arrogantly telling those who see better than us that they're blind and we're not.

Jesus came in contact with people just like us. And to those who were willing to acknowledge their blindness He gave sight. But those who refused to let Him guide them He left in their blindness.

Do you want to see? You may not even know you have any blind spots, yet all of us do. So before you go any further, enter into God's presence through prayer, asking the Holy Spirit to work on your spiritual eyes as you work through this chapter of our study. Then, when He shows you what you have tried to hide for so long, don't close your eyes to it. Instead, ask Him to give you strength to look at it for what it is and to depend on Him to help you deal with it honestly and honorably. That's a request He is delighted to answer.

A SEEING MIRACLE

As Jesus escaped being stoned, "He saw a man who was blind from birth" (John 9:1). Seeing this man, too, Jesus' disciples asked a question (v. 2). What does their question reveal about their concept of the cause of physical disabilities?

    BEHIND THE SCENES

Jesus' disciples were not alone in their belief about the cause of physical handicaps. Some Jewish texts of that day

taught that the soul of a person could sin in a preexistent
state (Wisdom 8:20). Many believed that a baby still in the
womb could have feelings, even sinful ones (cf. Gen. 25:22;
Luke 1:41–44). And it was widely held that Exodus 20:5 and
34:6, 7 taught that one's descendants would be punished for
one's sins. The disciples just wanted Jesus to resolve this
theological issue for them in regard to this blind man.[1]

Jesus' answer to His disciples doesn't resolve their theological inquiry. In fact, it doesn't say at all what caused this
man's blindness. All it does is say what can be done through it.
And what is that? (John 9:3–5)

FAITH ALIVE

It's very easy for us to speculate about why someone is
suffering. What better way does Jesus' response to His disciples pave for us on this matter?

How did Jesus heal this blind man? (vv. 6, 7)

Did the blind man have any assurances from Jesus that, if he
followed His directions, he would be healed?

What does this tell you about the role of faith in this miracle?

What relationship do you see between this miracle and Jesus' statement in verse 5?

What was the reaction of the healed man and those who personally knew him to this sign? (vv. 8–12)

A BLIND INTERROGATION

As you might expect, this man's incredible healing prompted an investigation and interrogation by—you guessed it—the Pharisees, the reigning legalists of the day (v. 13). Why were they so interested in this man? (vv. 14–16)

When their interrogation began, what divisive opinions did this man's opening testimony create among the Pharisees? (v. 16)

What was the healed man's initial conclusion about Jesus? (v. 17)

Not getting the answers they wanted, the Pharisees tried to rationalize away the miracle. What explanation for it did they offer and seek to prove? (v. 18)

Did they make their case stick when they interrogated the man's parents? (vv. 19–23) What happened?

How about when they recalled the healed man? Did he recant his earlier testimony, or did he strengthen it? Support your answer from the text (vv. 24–33).

Unable to make their case stick, what did the Pharisees do? (v. 34) Did they change their minds? repent? apologize?

True Sight vs. True Blindness

What happened between Jesus and the healed man after the Pharisees' interrogation? (vv. 35–38)

For what purpose did Jesus come into the world? (v. 39)

(Note: Remember that God's "judgment" is a boon of *deliverance* to those who trust Him, but a curse upon those who resist Him. Judgment, as in a lawsuit's resolution, works both ways.)

When some of the Pharisees overheard Jesus' words, they asked Him somewhat arrogantly if He was suggesting that they were blind to the truth (v. 40). After all, they were the strict teachers of the Law. If anyone knew the truth, they did. Jesus' reply is penetrating (v. 41) but at first blush enigmatic. "Jesus moved the discussion from physical blindness to spiritual blindness. To believe in Jesus means to see spiritually, whereas those who do not believe in Him remain blind,"[2] caught in the darkness of their own sin.

THE SHEPHERD'S WAY

Jesus didn't stop there. He continued to address the Pharisees, but this time through the imagery of shepherding rather than blindness and seeing. The Pharisees would have been very familiar with the shepherding illustration. This imagery is used throughout the Old Testament. Look up the following passages to gain some understanding of what the Pharisees could have linked Jesus' words to: Genesis 49:24; Psalm 23:1; 80:1; Isaiah 40:10, 11; 56:9–12; Jeremiah 23:1–4; 25:32–38; Ezekiel 34.

In Jesus' address to the Pharisees, He identifies Himself with two of the symbols He uses: He is the "door of the sheep" (John 10:7, 9) and the "good shepherd" (vv. 11, 14). The first image identification goes from verses 1–10, and it is set in contrast to a thief. The second image identification covers verses 11–18, and its opposite is the hireling, or hired hand. With this structure in mind, fill in the charts that follow, summarizing what Jesus says about Himself as the sheep door and good shepherd in contrast to the thief and hired hand.

THE SALVATION DOOR
(vv. 1–10)

THE SHEEP DOOR	THE THIEF

THE SAVIOR SHEPHERD
(vv. 11–18)

THE GOOD SHEPHERD	THE HIRED HAND

How did the Pharisees respond to Jesus' teaching? (vv. 19–21)

FAITH ALIVE

What life applications can you draw from Jesus' teaching in verses 1–18?

PLAIN TALK AND DEADLY STONES

Between John 7:1—10:21 and the confrontation recorded in 10:22–39 lies a period of about two months. The setting of the former passage is the Feast of Tabernacles, which was celebrated in October. The religious celebration at the center of the latter passage is the Feast of Dedication, which occurred in December.

BEHIND THE SCENES

"The Feast of Dedication, known today as Hanukkah, had its origin in the liberation and rededication of the temple under the Maccabeans in 165 B.C., after it had been desecrated by the Seleucid king Antiochus Epiphanes.[3]

Jesus once again entered the temple area in Jerusalem, but this time, while He was just walking about, the Jews encircled Him in an attempt to keep Him from escaping (vv. 23, 24). What did they want to know? (v. 24)

When had they raised this issue before? Flip back through the gospel to find out.

What did Jesus say to them? (vv. 25–30)

How did the Jewish authorities react and why? (vv. 31–33)

Given what His opponents thought Jesus was saying, He had the perfect opportunity to set them straight if they had misunderstood Him. But Jesus didn't do that. Instead, He offered an argument that further supported His claim to be one with the Father. Let's take a close look at His case.

First, Jesus quotes from Psalm 82:6 (John 10:34). The Psalm doesn't speak about false gods or deify humanity. What does it deal with? Read the entire Psalm in more than one translation. Who are the "gods"?

Second, in John 10:35, 36, Jesus argues that since the Scriptures cannot be broken—nullified or made void—and they refer to certain people as gods, then what's the problem with His referring to Himself as the Son of God, especially since He has a special relationship to the Father? What is that relationship?

Third, He's willing to rest His entire case for His unity with the Father on the fact that His miraculous works verify that unity (vv. 37, 38). In other words, if His claim to unity is false, how could they account for His ability to cure congenital blindness with spit and clay or to make lame men walk or to turn water into wine? And if such acts really are supernatural, then who but the Father could be their source? His Son, that's who!

How did the Jews respond to His argument? (v. 39)

Once again, Jesus escapes their trap.

WHERE THE BLIND REALLY SEE

After Jesus leaves Jerusalem, where does He go? (v. 40; cf. 1:28)

What do verses 41 and 42 say about John the Baptist's ministry?

After all the confrontation, deceit, hypocrisy, and tirades Jesus faced in Jerusalem, how do you think He felt when the common people in the countryside believed in Him by faith?

 FAITH ALIVE

How about you? Is your faith based on keeping certain religious formulas, traditions, or practices, on pleasing certain people, obeying certain moral codes, or on any other thing or duty? If confidence and convictions are not rooted in the tri-une God—Father, Son, and Holy Spirit—if anyone thinks to reach heaven or perfection or spiritual maturity through any other avenue, then they are dead wrong. Belief begins and is sustained forever in the Lord alone. No one nor anything else is sufficient. Is there any area of your life where this absolute dependence on Him needs to be asserted? Make sure you settle this matter with Him today.

1. J. Carl Laney, *John,* Moody Gospel Commentary, gen. ed. Paul Enns (Chicago, IL: Moody Press, 1992), 172; Merrill C. Tenney, "The Gospel of John," in *The Expositor's Bible Commentary,* gen. ed. Frank E. Gaebelein (Grand Rapids, MI: Zondervan Publishing House, 1981), 9:101.
2. *Spirit-Filled Life Bible* (Nashville, TN: Thomas Nelson Publishers, 1991), 1592, note on 9:35–41.
3. Ibid., 1594, note on 10:22.

Lesson 10/Giving Life and Predicting Death
(10:40—12:50)

To gain you must lose.
To rule you must serve.
To receive you must ask.
To learn obedience you must suffer.
To live you must die.
To die you must choose life.

On the surface these statements seem absurd, paradoxical, contradictory, illogical. But when you explore their depths you discover that they make perfect sense. Jesus proved them true in His own life.

He gave up His heavenly glory in order to regain it and enlarge it with the glorification of spiritual children such as you and me.

As the ruler over all, He became the model servant to all.

His earthly ministry led to the establishment of His church, but that could not have been done without the countless hours He spent before His Father in prayer.

As the Son of Man, He learned that the price tag of obedience has suffering written all over it.

He knew that the prelude to eternal bliss with the Father was temporary separation from the body through death.

He also understood that by committing Himself to serve the Father in life, He would have to die.

Jesus was no stranger to the hard realities of life. He faced them, worked through them, and always tried to bring good out of them. But He was not stoic about them. They impacted Him; they stirred up His feelings, His compassion, His anger, His love. We'll see this fact about Him very clearly in John 11 and 12. We'll see Him bring life out of death, but not before it evokes His tears and anger. We'll also see Him heralded as the king of Israel while He prepares to die at the hands of the Jewish leaders. And, if we'll look closely, we'll see in Him how we can deal with life's "paradoxes" and come out on top, even when it appears that the world has us down for good.

WHEN DEATH PRECEDES LIFE

John 11 opens with some bad news being delivered to Jesus. What was that news, and who sent it to Him? (vv. 1–3)

What did Jesus do when He received this disturbing news? (John 11:4–6) Why did He do this?

When Jesus announced that He wanted to return to Judea to "awaken" Lazarus (vv. 7, 11, 14, 15), how did the disciples respond? (vv. 8, 12, 13, 16) What were they concerned about? Were their worries justified?

 FAITH ALIVE

God's timetable is rarely in accord with ours because He usually wants to do something greater in our circumstances than we could ever imagine. Jesus could have gone to Bethany and healed Lazarus while he was still sick, but the Father had a different plan in mind. He wanted to show through His Son that He had authority over death, not just disease. And by doing so, He would be glorified, His Son would be, too, and generations upon generations would find eternal life instead of eternal death through the only Savior who can guarantee such an incredible gift.

What are you waiting on God to answer? Could the delay be for not only your good but for the well-being of countless others? Could it be that He will accomplish far more doing it His way and in His timing rather than in yours? Consider this carefully, and place your wholehearted trust in Him, asking Him to respond as He wills. Then watch out! His answer and timing will astound you.

WHEN LIFE OVERCOMES DEATH

By the time Jesus arrived near or in Bethany, He learned that Lazarus, His dear friend, had been dead for four days (v. 17). Before He reached Lazarus's home, Martha rushed out to see Him (v. 20). Recount the exchange that took place between them (vv. 21–27).

How do you think Martha's initial comments made Jesus feel? How would they have struck you?

FAITH ALIVE

Have you ever been blamed for causing a crisis or tragedy because you didn't act quickly enough? Whether you were at fault or not, it didn't feel good, did it? Jesus knows how you felt. He was also blamed by very close friends for letting someone He loved die.

If you've never shared those hurt feelings with Him, do so now. He wants to comfort you with knowing arms.

BEHIND THE SCENES

Martha's belief that Lazarus would "rise again in the resurrection on the last day" (v. 24) was very common in first-century Judaism. Almost all in the Jewish world (the exception being the Sadducees, Matt. 22:23; Mark 12:18) accepted the idea that at the end of the world, all humankind would be resurrected from the dead, unbelievers to divine condemnation and believers to divine blessing (Ps. 16:8–11; 73:23–26; Is. 26:14; Dan. 12:1–4). But the idea that the resurrection of an isolated individual could occur in history, before the world ended, was totally foreign to them. Consequently, Martha's confession in Jesus as the divine Messiah does not mean that she believed He would raise up Lazarus before the end of the age. What Jesus eventually did surprised even her.[1]

After Martha left Jesus, Mary went out to see Him (vv. 28–30). Who followed her? (vv. 31, 33; cf. v. 19)

What did Mary do when she saw Him? (v. 32)

How did Jesus react to this scene? (vv. 33–35)

What impact did His response have on others? (vv. 36, 37)

 FAITH ALIVE

Whether you are a man or a woman, you may have trouble expressing your emotions. Perhaps you're afraid of what others might think, or maybe you grew up in a home where emotions couldn't be expressed, only stifled. Whatever the reason, know that Jesus saw nothing wrong with letting deep feelings flow from His being for all to see. Remember, He created your ability to feel. Emotions are good. You don't need to hide them.

John 11:38–57 records what Jesus did next and how people reacted to the miracle and what He finally had to do.

BEHIND THE SCENES

The council that convened to discuss Jesus was the Sanhedrin (see p. 48). Caiaphas, who was the son-in-law of Annas (John 18:13), was the high priest who headed the Sanhedrin from A.D. 18 to A.D. 36. A Sadducee, he saw Jesus as a threat to Judea. If the people tried to make Jesus the Messiah-King, Rome would come down on the nation and destroy it, so Caiaphas urges political expediency—sacrifice Jesus for the preservation of the nation. Unknowingly, however, Caiaphas's choice of action is prophetic. Jesus' death will indeed be good for the nation, but not for its physical preservation—rather for its spiritual salvation.

FAITH ALIVE

How do you feel about death?

Does the account of Jesus' raising Lazarus from the grave help you deal better with death? Why?

How can the fact that Jesus is our guarantee of resurrection and everlasting life help us comfort others who are terminally ill or bereaving the death of a loved one?

A PREBURIAL ANOINTING

Less than a week before another Passover celebration in Jerusalem, Jesus leaves Ephraim and returns to Bethany. Whom does He join there, and what happens? (12:1–9)

WORD WEALTH

Spikenard (12:3): "A valuable and fragrant ointment derived from the dried roots of the herbal plant called nard. By the first century A.D. it was already being imported from its native India in alabaster boxes. Because of its costliness, spikenard was used only for very special occasions."[2]

Three hundred denarii (12:5): Roughly equivalent to a year's wages.

FAITH ALIVE

What precious possession would you be willing to sacrifice as a love-offering to Jesus? When and how will you give it up? Remember, this is not some legalistic requirement; such a gift should come out of a grateful heart. So give only if you really want to, and give out of a sense of deep thankfulness for the precious gift the Father has given you in His Son and Holy Spirit.

On the heels of this event, we're told that Jesus' life is not the only one in danger. Who else has been put on the religious leaders' hit list and why? (vv. 10, 11)

TRIUMPH AND TRAGEDY

As Jesus finally came closer to Jerusalem, the pilgrims who were gathered there for the Passover ran out to meet Him (v. 12; cf. 17, 18). What happened when they greeted Him? (vv. 13–15, 19)

Did Jesus' disciples understand the significance of what was happening? (v. 16)

BEHIND THE SCENES

Due to the signs Jesus had performed, especially the raising of Lazarus from the dead, the people were ecstatic to see Jesus coming to the Passover. Many had come to believe that He was the expected Messiah, but the Messiah they were looking for was a political one—a mighty Warrior-King who would lead them in battle against their enemies, achieving victory and reestablishing the independence of their nation. Their laying palm branches in the road before Jesus was a symbol of their nationalism and sense of impending victory. And their shouting *Hosanna,* which means "please save" or "save now" (cf. Ps. 118:25), and calling Him the Coming One and the King of Israel served only to reiterate their belief that He was entering the city as their political Savior.[3]

What happened next certainly confused those who expected a Messiah different from Jesus. In your own words, recount what took place (vv. 20–36).

How does the gospel writer explain the people's misperceptions of Jesus? (vv. 37–41)

What did Jesus finally shout to the crowd, even to those who believed in Him but kept silent out of fear and pride? (vv. 42–50)

FAITH ALIVE

Even in the midst of such incredible misperceptions, did Jesus give in, quit, and go home?

What can you learn from Jesus' example about how to handle stubborn unbelief, mistaken notions about Christianity, and even cowardly belief?

1. William L. Craig, *Knowing the Truth About the Resurrection,* rev. ed. (Ann Arbor, MI: Servant Books, 1988), 117–119.

2. *Spirit-Filled Life Bible* (Nashville, TN: Thomas Nelson Publishers, 1991), 1597, note on 12:3.

3. Edwin A. Blum, "John," in *The Bible Knowledge Commentary: New Testament Edition,* gen. eds. John F. Walvoord and Roy B. Zuck (Wheaton, IL: Victor Books, 1983), 317.

Lesson 11/Servant Power
(13:1—14:14)

We all know powerful people: presidents, congressional representatives, employers, pastors, teachers, business magnates, entrepreneurs, inventors, parents, even some children. Most of the powerful people around us love their power; they're infatuated with their influence over other people, policies, theories, properties—whatever it is they strive to control.

Jesus was also a powerful Person. Anyone who could create a universe out of nothing, sustain it by His word, and alter it at will has power beyond our wildest dreams. Of course, those activities belong to His deity. What about His humanity? How did He show and exercise power as a man? The answer is fascinating.

Jesus subjugated His power to the Father. His submission was so thorough that He could say that nothing He did, taught, or spoke came from Him. Everything He did, He did with the Father's prior direction and permission. Heal a paralytic or a blind man? No problem, as long as the Father gives the okay. Turn water into wine or raise a man from the dead? If the Father tells Him to, He'll do it. Tell the people that He is one with the Father even if that will enrage them? Yes, as long as the Father directs Him to do it. (Note John 5:19, 30; 7:16; 8:28, 29, for examples.)

What kind of power is this? The most potent power in the world—*servant power*. It can never be misused because it always obeys God. It will always accomplish what it's intended to because God will back it all the way. It will do only good, because the all-good God is its source, sustainer, guide, and goal. It can never be tyrannical, because its source is God; and He is always motivated by perfect love, because that's exactly what He is. It can never be defeated, because nothing in the universe can effectively compete with its all-powerful source. And Jesus had this power as no one has before or since. He was the Servant par excellence; He has no equal.

How can we tap into the power Jesus had? There's only one way—Jesus' way, which is the Father's way. John 13:1—14:14 tells us many of the basics, but John 14:15—16:33 tells us about the Helper who is necessary to make servant power an effective reality in our daily lives.

In this chapter, we'll start where Jesus does, with the basics.

KNOWLEDGE OF GOD'S WILL

Recall the setting. Jesus entered Jerusalem five days before the Passover feast to the cheers of those who thought He had come to deliver them from Roman oppression (12:1, 12, 13). He knew there was a price on His head, but He came anyway and preached the gospel.

As John 13 opens, the Passover feast has still not begun, but Jesus knows He is where He's supposed to be. What in the text indicates this? (vv. 1–3)

Jesus knew the Father's will. All through the gospel we see indications of that. What are some other passages you might cite?

 FAITH ALIVE

Do you know God's will? Are you spending sufficient time with Him, listening to His voice within, studying His written Word, seeking the counsel of godly men and women? He doesn't want to hide His will from you, but He does find it hard to find people who know how to listen. If you're not sure how to hear, ask Him to teach you. He's more than willing.

COMMITMENT

The second basic of servant power is also found in John 13:1. In addition to what Jesus knew, what did He do?

What else in the Fourth Gospel would support this statement? Try to name four or five pieces of evidence.

 ### FAITH ALIVE

How's your dedication to others? Are you dependable, even in crises? Do the members of your immediate and extended family know you will stick by them, no matter what? Do your friends? your church? work associates? What do you need to work on in terms of your commitment to others? As hard as it might be, you may get more objective answers to these questions if you ask them of some of the people you know from each of these groups. Remember, we all have blind spots.

HUMILITY

The third basic comes from an act Jesus performed at the last meal He had with His disciples, the evening before He would be executed. What did He do? (vv. 4–11)

What was the point of the exercise? (vv. 12–17)

FAITH ALIVE

What's your humility quotient? How willing are you to stoop down to do some things that you may even think are beneath you? Can you work behind the stage or must you always be in the spotlight? Do you take on some thankless tasks, not just those that bring high praise? Jesus said that blessing comes in doing, not mere knowing (v. 17). Are you willing to put self aside and serve others first for Christ's sake? Bare yourself before the Lord. Let Him handle your pride.

COURAGE

Another servant-power basic is conveyed in one of the most tragic sections of Scripture. Read verses 18–30. Put yourself in Christ's sandals. He spent more than three years building into the lives of the twelve disciples, knowing that a time would come when one of the Twelve would violate His trust and spit on His teaching and turn Him over to His enemies. Notice what He says, how He says it, the emotions He exudes, and how clueless the other disciples are, including the gospel's writer, John (the disciple "whom Jesus loved," v. 23). Record your thoughts.

FAITH ALIVE

What Jesus did took incredible courage. Without hedging or backing down, He put the wheels of His own betrayal into motion. Why? So the Father's will would be fulfilled, and through it His disciples would come to a firmer belief in Him as the predicted messianic God-man (vv. 18, 19).

Can you serve with that kind of courage? Are you willing to sacrifice all—your time, energy, plans, hopes, dreams, finances, possessions, relationships, even your life—for the

Lord and His work, if He so chooses? Would you even permit yourself to be betrayed for the sake of the kingdom? Pour out to God your fears, concerns, everything standing in your way of serving Him with selfless boldness and determination. Let Him work in your heart to increase your courage for Him.

LOVE

Once again, the Master sets the example and calls on us to copy Him. In essence, what does He say in verses 31–35?

FAITH ALIVE

Feelings may accompany love, but they should not be confused with the kind of love Jesus has for us and wants us to have toward each other. The love of which He speaks— *agape love*—is sacrificial, unconditional, constant, self-sustaining, always seeking the best of the other person. In Scripture, it's best described in 1 Corinthians 13:4–8.

Take each of the characteristics of love described there and ask yourself how your love compares. This exercise is not meant to produce guilt, but to show you how great servant love really is. Be honest before the Lord so He can better work in your life.

SERVANT LOVE IS . . .	MY LOVE IS . . .
Longsuffering	
Kind	
Not envious	
Self-effacing	
Not arrogant	

Courteous

Unselfish

Not irritable

Not resentful

Unhappy about evil

Joyful over the truth

All-supportive

All-accepting

All-hopeful

All-persevering

Unfailing

APPRECIATION FOR TIMING

In response to what Jesus said in John 13:33, Peter raises some questions that Jesus takes time to answer (vv. 36–38). Summarize Peter's questions as well as Jesus' responses.

Question 1:

Answer 1:

Question 2:

Answer 2:

 FAITH ALIVE

There are three ways you can miss the right time—arrive early, arrive late, or don't arrive at all. True servant power seeks to be used at just the right time; it doesn't rush ahead, lag behind, or hide.

Do you find yourself trying to push God's timetable a bit faster? Or do you find God urging you to pick up the pace? Or are you like Adam and Eve in the Garden of Eden, trying to hide from God altogether?

Jesus was at the center of the Father's will at all times. He knew when His hour had not arrived as well as when it came. This knowledge of and appreciation for God's timing kept Jesus moving at a steady, effective pace.

If that's what you long for, God is more than willing to help you experience it. Just ask. It's consistent with His will, so He'll be happy to answer your prayer.

BELIEF IN CHRIST AS GOD

Although Jesus' disciples had been with Him, seeing His miracles, hearing His teaching, receiving private lessons in theology and life, and observing firsthand the outworking of His compassion and convictions, they still didn't completely understand as they would need to. So, once again, Jesus went over who He was and what He had come to do.

Summarize the exchange that takes place in John 14:1–11.

 FAITH ALIVE

Belief in Christ as God is the fundamental of fundamentals. If that is false, so is Christianity. If it's true, and it definitely is, then Jesus really is "the way, the truth, and the life," and apart from Him there is no entryway to the Father. Is that truth a settled fact for you? If not, servant power will always remain elusive to you.

State your conviction about Christ here. If you have any doubts, ask the Lord and perhaps some knowledgeable friends to help you address them. This is critical. Don't put it off.

ASSURANCE OF SUPPORT

The last basic of servant power comes out in verses 12–14. What does Jesus say here?

 FAITH ALIVE

Jesus will help us do greater works than He did by manifesting His changeless mightiness through answered prayer. That's our assurance. He promised that He would not leave us to our own resources. We can draw upon His, and they are unlimited.

Do you avail yourself of this incredible promise and privilege? Do you seek to know His will, then ask Him to carry it out? He promised that He will not fail to answer such a prayer; the divine "Yes!" can echo constantly through the highs and lows of our lives. Make a list of areas where you would like to begin to see "greater things" worked by the Holy Spirit's power.

Now, if you haven't already, how about committing here—today—to making prayer a daily affair? Seek the Lord. Discern His will. Then pray for the accomplishing of His purposes. After that, watch Him say "Yes!" as your prayers release "greater works" according to His Word.

A GLANCE AHEAD

After assessing yourself against the basics, do you feel inadequate to the task? Does it seem that you could never meet the basic requirements, so servant power could never be a part of your experience? If you answered yes, you're not only being honest—you're absolutely correct. These basics are beyond the reach of all of us—IF we try to attain them in our own power. You see, servant power is really a gift, not an acquisition. And there's only one way to receive it: through Christ. We must first believe that He is the Son of God, the Savior of the world, our Deliverer, and we must put our trust in Him. Then, and only then, Jesus supplies the rest of what we need: the One He called the Helper. This One is the Holy Spirit, the Third Person of the Blessed Trinity. He empowers us to live as servants; without Him, our attempts at servanthood would be poor imitations of the real thing. He is the final key, the power key, and we'll learn more about Him in the next chapter.

So don't despair. God never commands us to do something without also giving us the ability to obey it. And in this case, our ability is wrapped up in the omnipotence of the Holy Spirit.

Lesson 12/The Divine Helper (14:15—16:33)

- "I can't figure out how to do this math problem. Mom, could you help me?"
- "If my boss jumps on me one more time, I'm going to quit. I don't need his criticisms—I need his help."
- "My husband isn't like a lot of other husbands I know. He really shares the load at home. If he didn't, I think both of us working at outside jobs would put too much of a strain on our marriage."
- "Both of my children love softball, but my younger daughter is catching on faster and starting to do a little better than her older sister, because her coach works the team harder and yet knows when to back off and praise their accomplishments. One time my older daughter said that she wished her coach was more like her sister's. I wish that, too."

We all need helpers. From the time we're conceived, we depend on an untold number of people to help provide us with food, shelter, clothing, financial security, education, employment, entertainment, spiritual understanding and growth . . . just about anything we need in life. Sometimes we live with the myth that we can become totally independent, resting solely on our abilities to get and do what we want. In reality, however, we are anything but independent; and we can never change that. None of us ever goes it alone or unaided; helpers surround us at every turn. Of course, we can get bad help or we can ignore or misuse the help we receive, but without a lot of assistance, not one of us would ever make it.

In fact, it's very likely that you can recall at least one helper who at some time kept you from going over the edge or who spurred you on to accomplish something or become someone you thought was out of reach. Maybe it was a coach or music teacher who made you practice until your craft became second nature and led you to heights you had known only in your dreams. Or maybe it was a parent who never gave up on you, even when you had given up on yourself. Perhaps your helper was a peer, a friend, who offered you a safe place where you could dream, complain, and find comfort and renewed strength. Whoever you point to, they had helpers, too—people who took them under their wings and gave them what they needed to soar.

God knows we need helpers—He designed us that way (cf. Gen. 2:18–24). We were created to need other people and God as well. And through His Son, the Father supplies us with the greatest, most reliable, powerful, knowledgeable, gifted Helper we have ever had or could ever receive—the Holy Spirit. But what is He like? How can He help us? How can He become a vital part of our lives? John 14:14—16:33 tells us, and that's the passage we're going to explore in this chapter.

But we're going to move through this section of Scripture a bit differently. Rather than taking the verses in order, we're going to approach them topically. This will help us experience a more systematic approach to their teaching.

ANOTHER HELPER

During His last supper with His disciples the night before His death, Jesus spoke a great deal about "another Helper." Consider what He said about this Helper in 14:16–18, 25, 26; 15:26; 16:5–15. These passages reveal a great deal about Him, including information about His nature, His work among believers and unbelievers, His relationship to the Father and the Son as well as to Christians and non-Christians, the timing of His arrival, and how He can be known and received. Record your discoveries in the left-hand column below. Then, in the right-hand column, record any comments you would like to make. These comments may be questions, points of application, observations, or anything else that comes to mind. The object is to interact with the text, to let it speak to you and to respond back. Remember, God's Word is living and active, not dead and impotent (Heb. 4:12), so give it an opportunity to enter into dialogue with you. The conversation will only help you.

THE HOLY SPIRIT AND ME

MY DISCOVERIES	MY COMMENTS
14:16–18	
14:15, 26	
15:26	
16:5–15	

 WORD WEALTH

Pray (14:16): A request made from an equal to an equal, unlike the Greek word translated *ask* in 14:13, 14, which concerns a request made by an inferior to a superior.[1]

Another (14:16): Distinct, but of the same kind. The Holy Spirit is a different Person from Christ but He is fully God as Christ is.

Helper (14:16): Aid, advocate, defender, friend at court, counselor, comforter, one who helps shoulder a heavy burden.[2]

Dwells with . . . in (14:17): This distinction points out the difference in the Holy Spirit's manner of work in the Old Testament and from Pentecost on. During the Old Covenant, the Holy Spirit was available to and present with some believers for selective purposes and only temporarily (Judg. 3:10; 6:34; 11:29; 13:25; 1 Sam. 16:14; Ps. 51:11). Under the New Covenant that Jesus ushered in through His death, resurrection, and ascension, the Spirit forever indwells all believers upon their initial confession of faith (Ezek. 36:27; Rom. 8:11; 1 Cor. 6:19; 12:13). Then, through welcoming His overflowing fullness, believers receive the Spirit's power for ministry, service, obedience and sanctification (Rom. 8:4).

Orphans (14:18): Those left without protectors or caregivers. Christ would come back to His disciples temporarily after His resurrection (John 14:19) but permanently through the presence and ministry of the promised Helper, the Holy Spirit.

Proceeds (15:26): Comes forth, sent. The Holy Spirit comes from the Father through the Son.

Convict (16:8): In this context, the Holy Spirit takes the world to court and presents convincing evidence proving that it is guilty before God on three counts: (1) its refusal to believe in Christ, which shows the gravity of its sin; (2) its refusal to accept Christ as the perfect standard of righteousness, even though His ascension to the Father and the Father's acceptance of Him vindicate His righteous standing; (3) its refusal to accept liability for its impending judgment, which is proved certain because its spirit-ruler, Satan, stands judged before God already.

 FAITH ALIVE

There's a lot of material here for application, but let's just concentrate on three of the key points that surface.

First, Jesus said He would pray. Yes, He would approach the Father as an equal, but in His humanity He would depend on prayer to let His request be known. How is your prayer life? Do you pray daily, a few times a week, only in crises or at church? How committed are you to prayer? What do you pray about? Do you just zero in on your own needs or on the needs of your immediate family? If the Son of Man needed to pray, how much more do we! Write about your prayer life below, and note ways you can improve and grow in it. Prayer life is essential to the Christian life.

Second, the Holy Spirit was given to benefit us for the sake of Christ. How do you show your appreciation of that fact? Do you listen to the Spirit? talk to Him? obey Him? approach each day in His strength and with His wisdom? What role do you allow the Spirit to play in your everyday life? Do you employ His assistance in daily "prayer in the Spirit"? (Jude 20) Does He need to increase and you decrease? Share your thoughts here, perhaps even setting them out in a prayer to the Spirit. He's waiting to hear from you.

Third, the Holy Spirit's job is to convict the world; it is not our job. We don't need to make people feel bad, guilty, sinful, responsible, or anything else along those lines. The Holy Spirit is perfectly capable of handling that task. Our job is to share the good news, to tell people how they can find help to deal with their guilt. The bad news is handled by the Spirit of truth. And that's a good thing. Who are we, sinners ourselves, condemning others—pointing out their sins? That could make us sound self-righteous—in fact, we may even start thinking that we're better than other sinners. No. We are sinners telling other sinners where they can find forgiveness. That's great news!

How do you share the gospel? As a fellow struggler or as a judge and jury? Do you point a bony finger of blame or reach out a hand of merciful help? Be sure to go beyond thinking about your current approach and attitudes in witnessing and reflect on what you can do to improve both, leaving the Spirit to do His job while you do yours.

OBEDIENT LOVE

Jesus also talked a lot about love in 14:15, 21–24; 15:9–14, 17. As you read these verses, answer the following questions. You may discover some surprising things about love.

Who is loved and by whom?

How is love exercised?

What does love bring?

What Lover and love relationship should be our model?

How can we know if love is not present?

 FAITH ALIVE

What struck you about what these verses say about love? How might you love differently as a result?

THE ESSENTIAL SOURCE

One of the most famous sections of Jesus' last-supper talk concerns a vinedresser, a vine, its branches, and fruit. Take a look at John 15:1–8 and jot down what you learn about each of these images, their meaning, and significance.

THE VINEYARD

THE VINEDRESSER	THE VINE	THE BRANCHES	THE FRUIT

 BEHIND THE SCENES

The vine is one of the Old Testament images used to depict Israel (Ps. 80:8–16; Is. 5:1–7; Jer. 2:21; 5:10; 12:10; Ezek. 15:1–8; 17; Hos. 10:1). When Jesus uses this imagery in John's gospel, it is to identify Himself as the true Israel, the One who fulfills what the nation of Israel failed to do.

FAITH ALIVE

What is your relationship to the Vine? Are you really committed to Him or just playing around?

How is your relationship with Him? You can measure it by the fruit you're manifesting, and the fruit is Christlikeness brought about through the work of the Holy Spirit. Turn to Galatians 5:16–26 and consider what it says about the works of the flesh and the fruit of the Spirit. Which characterize your experience and how much? Remember, don't just think about outward behavior and achievements but also inward attitudes, motivations, thoughts, and beliefs.

If you find yourself falling short of abundant fruitfulness, that's okay. Fruit-bearing takes time; it's a process, one that God is committed to see you through. Your job is to abide in Christ, to stay by His side no matter what, seeking to obey Him through the empowerment of the Holy Spirit. The Spirit will handle the rest.

MORE THAN PRAYER

What Jesus says about prayer in John 14:13, 14, He briefly expands upon in 15:7, 14–16, but He does it with a different emphasis. In John 14, the focus is on the assurance of our prayers being answered as long as they are made in Christ's name (that is, according to His purpose and will). In John 15, however, the relationship of the one who prays to Christ is the focus. What do these verses say about this relationship and its importance to our prayers?

WHY BAD THINGS HAPPEN TO GOD'S PEOPLE

Jesus also spoke about hatred and persecution. He never told us that the Christian life would be free of pain or chaos; rather, He warned us that such would come because we identify ourselves with Him, the Light, and the world who has embraced the darkness cannot tolerate the Light, so the world fights against it, trying to snuff it out. Whether we like it or not, we are combatants, and the battle is unrelenting and brutal.

Note what Jesus says about it (John 15:18–25; 16:1–4), summarizing your thoughts about it here.

FAITH ALIVE

God's people will suffer persecution because of their devotion to Christ—that's indisputable. History bears out the truth of that statement, and if your experience hasn't proved it yet, it undoubtedly will, at least if you are standing for Him, bearing fruit through His Spirit.

Have you suffered for your commitment to Christ? First Peter was written expressly for believers who were facing persecution. Take some time out to read through that great letter. It will provide some helpful counsel and comfort that you're sure to turn back to time and time again. Feel free to jot down those thoughts that you will want to remember when persecution strikes.

THE COME-BACK LORD

Several times throughout this section in John's gospel Jesus talks about going away and returning. Look up these verses and summarize what they say in the space provided. Be sure to indicate what you think Jesus is talking about—in other words, what His words mean. Also observe what Jesus says He will give to believers in His physical absence.

14:16–21

14:22–31

15:26, 27

16:5–28

WORD WEALTH

Judas (14:22): Not the disciple who betrayed Jesus but the son of James (cf. Luke 6:16; Acts 1:13).

My Father is greater than I (14:28): This does not contradict Jesus' other statements that He is equal with the Father in deity; rather, it reaffirms that "he who is sent [is not] greater than he who sent him" (13:16). As the Father's messenger, Jesus serves Him and must give an account to Him for how well He has carried out His mission.

FAITH ALIVE

Jesus' resurrection is the most monumental and joyous event in all of biblical history. It demonstrates Christ's victory over sin, death, and Satan. When you add to that His ascension into heaven to rule with the Father's authority until all the power of His enemies has been vanquished, you realize that on Jesus' side, we are definitely on the winning side, endowed with the promised power of His Spirit and with every reason to expect His victory day by day.

In the last chapter of this study guide, we will zero in on Jesus' resurrection in much more detail, but given what Jesus says about it here in this passage of John's gospel, what applications for your life can you draw out? Be as specific as you can.

PROPHECY AND PEACE

To Jesus' closing words in John 16:25–28, Jesus' disciples made some final remarks (vv. 29, 30). What did they say?

What was our Lord's response? (vv. 31–33)

 FAITH ALIVE

As you considered these last few verses, what struck you as relevant to your situation?

1. J. Carl Laney, *John*, Moody Gospel Commentary, gen. ed. Paul Enns (Chicago, IL: Moody Press, 1992), 261.

2. Ibid.; Fritz Reinecker, *Linguistic Key to the Greek New Testament*, ed. Cleon L. Rogers, Jr. (Grand Rapids, MI: Zondervan Publishing House, 1980), 251; F. F. Bruce, *The Gospel of John* (Grand Rapids, MI: William B. Eerdmans Publishing Company, 1983), 301.

Lesson 13/*The Prayer of a Lifetime* (17:1–26)

Asking is such a simple thing. It begins with a need or a desire that we can't or would rather not fulfill ourselves. Then it looks for the person or persons who can make the fulfillment of that need or desire a reality, and it approaches them with the request. The approach can take a variety of forms: a candlelight dinner, a moonlit drive, a business meeting, a fishing expedition, a mountain hike, a game of chance or strength. Then, with the setting established, the method decided, the request is made.

Most of what we ask concerns ourselves. We want to know if our wants can be met. The second largest area of our asking concerns those individuals we really care about. Beyond that, we usually don't go far, unless, of course, it's to ask about fulfilling the needs of some cause we hold dear, and those causes are often special to us because something in our life or our loved ones' lives happened to endear them to us.

Believe it or not, Jesus' asking was in many ways just like ours. He, too, asked for His needs and desires to be fulfilled, and He wanted His loved ones and favorite causes to benefit, too. But the biggest differences between His asking and ours is (1) His requests were always wrapped up in the will of His Father, seeking to match exactly what His Father wanted; (2) His askings were always other-centered—even when they benefited Him, they were motivated by the overwhelming desire to benefit others first. Jesus asked perfectly, wisely, benevolently, unselfishly.

But more incredible than this—Jesus asked! The Lord of all, Sustainer of all, Creator of all, Owner of all . . . asked. He placed Himself in the most humble position—that of a needy, dependent person, and, like us, He asked. In doing so, He raised asking to a new level of dignity and sanctity. This simple, humble, commonplace activity is now special, even holy. Or at least it can be beyond what we could ever imagine.

The longest recorded section of Jesus' asking is found in John 17. Except for a very brief introduction, His asking takes up the entire chapter. And it occurs in the form of a prayer to His heavenly Father. As we'll see, this prayer is the prayer of a lifetime. It capsulizes not only what Jesus found to be most important but what we should as well. Our askings can never go wrong if they are centered on this prayer. Jesus prays the Father's will. That's a sure guarantee that His prayer will be answered. If we want our requests to God answered, we must pray according to His will. So let's discover what that is. Jesus will show us, and His Spirit will impress it on our minds and hearts. Let those who have ears to hear, listen.

THE DIRECTION

Some people pray sitting, others on bent knees, some standing, while others lie prostrate. The position is not nearly as important as the direction. Where do you look to have your prayer fulfilled? Jesus left no doubt what His direction was. What does the text say about this? (17:1)

 FAITH ALIVE

Whether you close your eyes when you pray or keep them open or physically look at a picture, scenery, or the floor makes no difference. What counts is where you look to find the Lord. If a person looks to nature because he or she sees God diffused throughout it like a vapor filling a container, that's not the God Jesus knew! Looking for Him within one's psyche, will, or emotions isn't the prayer style of Jesus either. For our Savior the Father to whom He prayed was and is reigning in heaven, draped in glorious splendor. That is the God He looked to.

What is your concept of God? Where do you look for Him?

Does the God to whom you pray accord with Jesus' understanding?

THE INTIMACY

Read through the entire seventeenth chapter of John, circling the titles Jesus used to refer to God. What are they? What do they tell you about the relationship Jesus and the Father shared?

WORD WEALTH

Holy (17:11): Separate from all that is sinful and defiling and common.

Righteous (17:25): Does what is right and just (cf. Ps. 119:137; Jer. 12:1).

FAITH ALIVE

Romans 8:14–17 tells us that, in Christ and through the Holy Spirit, we can enjoy the privileges of sonship that Jesus did, including the rich, loving intimacy. If you haven't approached the Lord with that kind of intimacy before, try so now. He wants you to come to Him as a trusting child.

THE FOCUS

Who did Jesus pray for, and in what order? The references that follow will tell you.

17:1–5

17:6–19

17:20–26

 FAITH ALIVE

What implications could His focus have on yours when you pray?

THE REQUESTS

In this prayer, Jesus made six requests of His Father, and He joined each one with a reason, a purpose, or a goal. See if you can identify them as you look up the following verses.

JESUS' PETITIONS

	HIS REQUESTS	HIS REASONS
17:1–3, 5		
17:11		
17:15, 16		

17:17–19

17:20, 21

17:24

FAITH ALIVE

What do these requests tell you about Jesus' desires and motivations? In what ways can you apply this information to your prayer life?

THE REPORTS

Jesus never forgot that He was on a mission for His Father. He used this prayer to report His accomplishments and ongoing work in regard to this mission. In other words, He didn't just ask, He also told. What did He say?

JESUS' TELLINGS

	WHAT'S BEEN DONE	WHAT'S BEING DONE	WHAT WILL BE DONE
17:4			
17:9–11			

17:12

17:13

17:14

17:18

17:19

17:20

17:22, 23

17:25, 26

FAITH ALIVE

If you had to report to the Father, what would you tell Him? What have you done for Him? What are you doing for Him? What else do you want to do for Him? Talk with your Father about these things. He's waiting to hear from you.

Lesson 14/From Grave to Glory (18:1—21:25)

Ask some non-Christians why they believe in life after death, and listen closely to their answers. Although their degree of assurance in postdeath existence will go from sheer disbelief to absolute certainty, what they believe about that life and why they believe it will boggle your mind.

Many unbelievers think that ghosts are evidence of life beyond the grave. For them, that kind of life is still earthly but bodiless and weightless. You can appear and reappear at will, float through solid objects, and glide through the air, but earth is still your home.

Others think that reincarnation theories are the best explanations. We are born, live, die, then return and repeat the cycle perhaps hundreds of thousands of times. We could come back as animals or humans, as paupers or billionaires—it all depends on how our good deeds balance against our bad deeds in each life. What's the evidence for all this? The most popular form is memory recall: the living person has memories that correspond to details of the deceased person's life. Once again, the life-after-death existence is earthbound, and this time it is physical.

Many other views abound, too, and the evidences usually cited for those are just as flimsy and subjective as the positions they allegedly support.

Well, then, what about the Christian view of the other side of death? Does it fare any better? Yes. In fact, the evidence is so great that it's almost embarrassing. And virtually all of it hinges on one event in biblical history: Jesus rising bodily alive and immortal from the dead. So essential is this event that the apostle Paul argued, "If Christ is not risen, your faith *is* futile; you are still in your sins! Then also those who have fallen asleep in Christ have perished. If in this life only we have hope in Christ, we are of all men the most pitiable" (1 Cor. 15:17–19).

This incredible, historically confirmed miracle is recorded in John's gospel, as well as in the other three gospels. In our last chapter in this study, we will see the final events leading up to this miracle, and we will also learn how Jesus confirmed the miracle to His disciples. He predicted that He would lay down His own life and raise it up again (John 2:19; 10:17, 18). John records the fulfillment of this, the seventh and greatest sign.

 ## BIBLE EXTRA

As you work through what follows, you may want to compare John's account of these events with what the other gospel writers record (Matt. 26:36—28:20; Mark 14:32—16:20; Luke 22:39—24:53). None of them provides a comprehensive account, so the comparisons can enrich your understanding of Jesus' betrayal, trials, death, burial, resurrection, postresurrection appearances, and ascension.

BETRAYED

John 18 records Judas Iscariot carrying out what Scripture had said he would do (vv. 1–12). Retell this event in your own words.

Why do you think the arresting authorities "drew back and fell to the ground" when Jesus said "I am *He*"? (v. 6; cf. 8:58, 59)

WORD WEALTH

Brook Kidron (18:1): This brook, "often dry in summer but rain-swollen in winter, runs along the eastern side of Jerusalem, past the Garden of Gethsemane and the Mt. of Olives. One coming from Jerusalem had to cross the Kidron to reach Gethsemane."[1] See also 2 Samuel 15:23, 30, 31.

The cup (18:11): The Old Testament associates God's cup with sorrow and judgment (Ps. 75:8; Is. 51:17; Jer. 25:15; Ezek. 23:31–34). The image may also indicate Jesus' bearing human sin and estrangement from the Father (Matt. 27:46; 2 Cor. 5:21).

FAITH ALIVE

Jesus was so committed to carrying out the Father's will that when Peter tried to defend Him, He stopped him and reminded Peter of what He had to do.

How committed are you to doing God's will? Talk to Him about it.

THE FIRST INTERROGATION

The text says that before being taken to Caiaphas, Jesus was led before Caiaphas's father-in-law, Annas (John 18:13). Even though Caiaphas was the high priest officially appointed and recognized by the Roman authorities of that time, Annas had served as high priest before him. The Jews regarded the high priestly office as a lifetime position, so for them, Annas was still the senior official.

What happened when Jesus appeared before Annas? (vv. 19–24)

FAITH ALIVE

Jesus was humiliated and unfairly treated by those who should have known who He was and welcomed Him as the Messiah. If you have ever been dealt with unjustly, know that Jesus understands exactly what you experienced and how you felt. Are you being mistreated now? Go to Him and tell Him about it. Don't hold anything back. He understands, and He's waiting to comfort you.

Notice, too, Jesus' defense. He was able to appeal to His ministry as being above reproach. How about yours? If charged with misconduct, could you make the same defense and make it stick?

DENIED

During Annas's interrogation of Jesus, one of Jesus' closest disciples denied he had ever known Him. Who was it? (v. 15)

Which other disciple was with Jesus at the time, and where were they? (v. 15; cf. 13:23; 19:25–27)

To whom did this disciple make his first denial? (vv. 16, 17)

His second denial? (vv. 18–25)

His third? (vv. 26, 27)

What is the significance of his denials and the rooster's crowing after the last one? (v. 27; cf. 13:37, 38)

FAITH ALIVE

It's an awful feeling to have a close friend turn on you, especially when you need him or her the most. Jesus knows that feeling well. Let Him apply that understanding to you when your friends fail you.

IN A PAGAN PALACE

The religious leaders had finally gotten their hands on Jesus and they weren't about to let Him go. After taking Him before Caiaphas where He was officially charged with blasphemy and sentenced to death (18:28; cf. Matt. 26:57–68), they marched Him off to the Praetorium so they could present a case against Him to Pilate.

BEHIND THE SCENES

When Judea became a Roman imperial province in A.D. 6, Pontius Pilate was appointed by the emperor as the prefect, or governor, of the province. He served in this capacity until A.D. 36. Although his permanent residence was in Caesarea (Acts 23:23, 24), Pilate stayed in Jerusalem during Jewish festival days so he was readily available to deal with crises and maintain order.

Ancient historians record that Pilate was a greedy, inflexible, and cruel leader hated by the Jews. In the case of Jesus, however, the Jewish authorities were willing to lay their hatred toward Pilate aside in order to exercise their greater hatred toward Jesus. You see, they could not carry out the death penalty under Roman law, but Pilate could. So they appealed to him to execute their vengeance.[2]

When they brought Jesus to the Praetorium—the Roman governor's official residence—they wouldn't go inside "lest they should be defiled, but that they might eat the Passover" (John 18:28). Jewish tradition held that the dwellings of Gentiles were unclean, and so the Passover could not be observed by those who were ceremonially defiled. This verse poses a chronological problem. The other three gospels record that Jesus ate the Passover with His disciples on Thursday evening and was crucified the next day, Friday. John's gospel, however, says that the Jews had not eaten the Passover yet even though it records earlier that Jesus and His disciples had already eaten the Passover lamb. What's going on?

Several solutions have been proposed, but the one that fits all the data the best is supplied by New Testament scholar Harold Hoehner.[3] He presents evidence that suggests the Jews celebrated two Passovers during Jesus' time because of two different ways of reckoning the day. One way was to reckon a day from sunrise to sunrise, which was the method used by Jesus and the gospel writers, excluding John, and it was likely followed in Galilee. The other way was to determine a day from sunset to sunset, which seems to have been the official Jewish method followed by John and the Judeans. Therefore, if this hypothesis is right, Jesus and His disciples observed the Passover on Thursday with the Galileans, while the Judean Jews, which would have included the religious authorities in Jerusalem, sacrificed their Passover lambs Friday afternoon.

 FAITH ALIVE

We often find it amazing that when the Truth was standing in front of Pilate, he asked what truth was. But how often do people do that today, even we, those who claim to know Him? We can know what's true and right and still fail to acknowledge it or follow it.

How are you and the Truth getting along? Do you really believe Him when He speaks? Do you really strive to follow Him wherever He may lead? Many of us don't, though we know we should, so don't feel embarrassed to come before Him and confess your confusion or fear or whatever else is holding you back from obeying Him fully. Let Him minister to you in your struggle. He wants to give you rest.

THE JUDGE IS JUDGED

In an attempt to pacify the religious leaders without giving in to their death-penalty demand, Pilate ordered that Jesus be "scourged" (19:1; cf. Luke 23:16).

 WORD WEALTH

Scourged (19:1): "A victim to be scourged was stripped and tied to a whipping post. Then he was beaten mercilessly with a whip consisting of several leather thongs, each loaded with jagged pieces of metal or bone and weighted at the end with lead. Fragments of flesh would be torn from the victims, some of whom did not survive the ordeal."[4]

After being further beaten and mocked by the Roman soldiers, Jesus was brought back out to the waiting Jewish authorities. Pilate hoped that the punishment Jesus had received would be enough to appease them even though Pilate himself still believed that Jesus was innocent of any wrongdoing (vv. 2–5). What happened when the religious leaders saw Jesus? (vv. 6, 7)

What happened between Pilate and Jesus after that? (vv. 8–11)

Once again, Pilate tried to release Jesus, but what was the response? (vv. 12–16)

WORD WEALTH

The one who delivered Me to you has the greater sin (19:11): More than likely, this statement refers to Caiaphas, not to Judas Iscariot. Because Caiaphas was the head of the religious establishment, having the greater responsibility to know and apply the Hebrew Scriptures with understanding and integrity, he bore the greater sin in relationship to Pilate, who had none of these advantages and privileges.

Not Caesar's friend (19:12): There was a club, an elite fraternity, called *Amici Caesaris*, the Friends of Caesar. Only high officials in the Roman Empire and some members of the Roman Senate were privileged to join, and no one left the club except under mortal disgrace. By throwing out this charge, the religious leaders were threatening to appeal to the emperor, pointing out to him that one of his closest confidants condoned treason by freeing a Man who had set Himself up as a subversive counter-king to Rome.[5]

The Pavement (19:13): "A raised platform upon which Pilate sat in judgment. Archaeologists identify it with an excavated Roman pavement that formed the courtyard of the Tower of Antonia."[6]

FAITH ALIVE

Ultimately our decision to follow Christ comes down to who we are going to serve—ourselves and our own concerns and agendas or Him and what He wants and requires. Are you facing a decision where you have to make this choice? Pilate made his—he chose to protect himself. What will your choice be?

MISSION ACCOMPLISHED

The account of Jesus' crucifixion is anything but pretty, but it is a record of what had to happen in order for Him to accomplish His mission for the Father and for us. So read it reverently, putting yourself at the scene. Let yourself see and touch the surroundings, hear and feel the anger, pain, and confusion. Don't let any detail pass by you. Remember, Jesus did this out of love—the purest, most precious love there could ever be. See if you can't understand it that way, and let the Holy Spirit do the rest.

WORD WEALTH

Crucified (19:18): Crucifixion was a shameful, agonizing, and very public death most often reserved for non-Roman slaves and revolutionaries. The victim's arms and legs were attached by ropes or spikes to a rough wooden cross that was planted upright into the ground for all to see. The cross itself could be a single post or stake, the traditional cross that formed a *t*, posts crossed to form an *X*, or a post with a cross-beam making a *T*. Without any body support, or perhaps a little for the victim's feet or seat, he would slowly die from muscular spasms and asphyxiation. Death could come about in several hours or take several days.

Sour wine (19:29): The ordinary drink of common laborers and soldiers. It relieved thirst better than water, and it was less expensive than regular wine. Giving Jesus this drink was not cruel but merciful.[7]

Hyssop (19:29): "A member of the mint family, a shrub-like plant"[8] the leaves of which were used in rituals of cleansing (Ex. 12:22; Lev. 14:4; Num. 19:6, 18).

CONFIRMATION AND BURIAL

After Jesus gave up His own life (John 19:30), His death was verified. How and by whom? (vv. 31–37)

FAITH ALIVE

Here, as well as several other times in this account, you have read about these events happening according to the prophecies of Jesus or Scripture (vv. 36, 37; cf. 18:31, 32; 19:24, 28). These affirm that whatever God says we can trust. He's never wrong; His word never fails. It could not be otherwise, because as the Truth and the omniscient One, He cannot lie or be wrong about anything. It's absolutely impossible (Titus 1:2; Heb. 6:17, 18).

Are you struggling with believing something He says? If you understand His words correctly, you need not worry whether they are true or whether He will ensure their accomplishment. He will—undoubtedly! Just trust Him and step out believing. He won't let you down.

After crucifixion, the Romans usually left the victims hanging, exposed to beasts of prey, which was the final humiliation. But preparations were made for Jesus' burial so He wouldn't suffer this fate. Note the account of His burial (John 19:38–42; cf. Luke 23:50–56) and jot down your observations.

HE'S ALIVE!

Jesus was crucified and buried on a Friday. From all appearances, it looked as though the movement He had begun died with Him. The religious leaders had won. Satan had defeated Him.

But the last word had not been spoken yet. Early Sunday morning, Mary Magdalene, one of the women who had watched Jesus die and who may have helped bury Him (Mark 15:47), arrived at His tomb, expecting, no doubt, to complete what had been hurried burial proceedings (Mark 16:1). What happened when she got there? What did she discover, and how was her discovery confirmed? (John 20:1—21:23)

WORD WEALTH

The first day of the week (20:1): This was Sunday, but not just any Sunday. The first Sunday after the Passover was the day when the Jews celebrated the Feast of Firstfruits. "The firstfruits are the first ripened part of the harvest, furnishing actual evidence that the entire harvest is on the way. According to Leviticus 23:4–14, the firstfruits in connection with the Passover were used to consecrate the coming harvest. Jesus died on the Passover, and His resurrection is a promise of our own resurrection."[9]

From this account of Jesus' resurrection and appearances, what indications are there that the followers of Christ didn't expect to see Him alive again?

How did Jesus verify to them that He had really risen from the dead in the same body in which He had died and been buried?

What was Jesus' message to Mary Magdalene? (20:15–17)

What did He tell the disciples during His first appearance to them? (vv. 19–23)

During His second visit? (vv. 24–29)

One of the most priceless examples of forgiveness and restoration in Jesus' ministry is found in 21:15–19. In your own words, describe what happens.

WORD WEALTH

Love . . . love (21:15, 16, 17): The word Jesus uses for *love* the first two times is *agape*, meaning unconditional, total devotion. The third time He uses the word for *love* that Peter does—*phileo*—which carries the ideas of affection, cherish, take pleasure in. After the three times Peter had denied Jesus, he wasn't prepared to make the commitment of *agape* love, so he offered all he thought he could give. Jesus apparently accommodated to that when He used Peter's word choice for *love* in His third question to Peter.

KEEP YOUR FOCUS

After Jesus made it clear to Peter that his service would eventuate in his death (vv. 18, 19), Peter asked Him what John's service would cost him (vv. 20, 21). What did Jesus tell Peter? (vv. 22, 23)

FAITH ALIVE

While serving Christ, it's so easy to get distracted, to get caught up with what other people are doing and how God is dealing with them in contrast to us. But Jesus' words to Peter should say as much to us as they did to him. Our focus should be on what God calls us to do, not on what He requires of others. How's *your* focus?

ALL THIS IS TRUE

How would you sum up John's last words? (vv. 24, 25)

FAITH ALIVE

No matter what else is said about the gospel story, the bedrock is that the story is true. Jesus came into human history, ministered in a flesh-and-blood body to real people, suffered, died, was buried, and rose again from the grave, conquering death forever. It all happened. We have eyewitness accounts affirming the veracity of these events and many more that haven't even been recorded. Jesus is not a fantasy, a wish-fulfillment, a legend concocted by people who desperately wanted to believe in someone who could guarantee their immortality. We have the best evidence in the world that all this is absolutely true. Our faith really is founded on fact. We don't have to leap into the abyss of incredulity.

By supplying us with such strong historical documents which archaeologists and Bible scholars have verified time and time again, God is telling us that He has no problems with our checking things out. He welcomes it. He has nothing to hide and so much to give.

But all the facts in the world won't save anyone until they put their trust in the One to whom history testifies. If you haven't already, come and put your trust in Him—either to receive everlasting life or to walk more closely with Him; it doesn't matter. He welcomes all who come to Him by faith exclaiming as Thomas did, "My Lord and my God!"

And as He may have already been received by you as your Savior and Lord—go forward, praising Him for power to live for His glory, beyond the ordinary!

1. *Spirit-Filled Life Bible* (Nashville, TN: Thomas Nelson Publishers, 1991), 1608, note on 18:1.

2. J. Carl Laney, *John,* Moody Gospel Commentary, gen ed. Paul Enns (Chicago, IL: Moody Press, 1992), 326, 327.

3. Harold Hoehner, *Chronological Aspects of the Life of Christ* (Grand Rapids, MI: Zondervan Publishing House, 1977), chap. 4.

4. *Spirit-Filled Life Bible,* 1460, 1461, note on 27:26.

5. Paul L. Maier, *In the Fullness of Time: A Historian Looks at Christmas, Easter, and the Early Church* (San Francisco, CA: HarperCollins, 1991), 161.

6. *Spirit-Filled Life Bible* (Nashville, TN: Thomas Nelson Publishers, 1991), 1610, note on 19:13.

7. Laney, *John,* Moody Gospel Commentary, 349.

8. *Spirit-Filled Life Bible,* 99, note on 12:22.

9. Ibid., 1743, note on 15:20.